Traumatic Cognitive Dissonance

Healing From An Abusive Relationship With A Disordered Personality

Peter Salerno, PsyD

First Edition

The Library of Congress has cataloged this paperback edition. Publication data available upon request.

ISBN 979-8-9919755-1-3 (paperback)

Printed in the United States

The information in this book is intended for general inquiry and informational purposes only and should not be utilized as a substitute for medical advice, diagnosis, or treatment. If you think you or those under your care are ill or in need of health care of any kind, please seek immediate medical attention. Always consult with a doctor or other competent licensed clinical professional for specific recommendations about medical treatments for yourself or those under your care. Any use of, or reliance in any way upon, the information contained in this book is solely at your own risk.

The author has checked with sources believed to be reliable in his efforts to provide information that is complete and generally in accord with the standards of practice that are accepted at the time of publication. However, in view of the possibility of human error or changes in behavioral, mental health, or medical sciences, neither the author nor any other party who has been involved in the preparation or publication of this work warrants that the information contained herein is in every respect accurate or complete, and they are not responsible for any errors or omissions, or the results obtained from the use of such information. Readers are encouraged to confirm the information contained in this book with other sources.

CONTENTS

SECTION 1
RECOGNITION

SECTION 2
IDENTIFICATION

SECTION 3
RECOVERY

About the Author

Peter Salerno, PsyD, LMFT, is a licensed psychotherapist and award-winning author. He holds a Doctor of Psychology degree (PsyD), a Master of Science degree (MS) in Clinical Psychology, and a Bachelor of Arts (BA) degree in English Literature. Dr. Salerno is a trauma specialist, clinical supervisor, and consultant who utilizes empirically validated, science-based approaches to promote healing and self-empowerment. Dr. Salerno is trained in Eye Movement Desensitization and Reprocessing Therapy (EMDR) and is certified in Family Trauma and Complex Trauma through the International Association of Trauma Professionals. He also holds certifications in Psychoanalytic Psychotherapy and Personality Disorder Treatment (C-PD) and is trained and qualified to administer and score the Hare Psychopathy Checklist-Revised (PCL-R). Dr. Salerno has treated mental health conditions in a variety of clinical settings and has authored six books on a broad number of topics, including stress and trauma, early development and attachment, mind-body integration, emotion and cognition, personality pathology, and philosophy. His book, "The Nature and Nurture of Narcissism," was the #1 new release on Amazon in its category, and his book, "Fit For Off Duty" is now required reading for law enforcement officers at the FBI Academy, which is the Federal Bureau of Investigation's training and research center for FBI agents in Quantico, Virginia. Dr. Salerno currently works in private practice in California and consults internationally for educational purposes. He also facilitates virtual educational workshops on a regular basis for individuals who have experienced traumatic cognitive dissonance as a result of pathological relationship abuse.

Website: drpetersalerno.com
Email: peter@drpetersalerno.com
Instagram: @drpetersalerno
YouTube: @DrPeterSalerno

Dedication

For all the incredibly brave individuals from around the world who have reached out to me and shared their survival stories. Your courage is truly inspiring, and you can and will heal.

Preface

When I became a therapist, I didn't intentionally set out to dedicate my entire career to deep diving into personality science and personality disorder research. I didn't set out to specialize in helping victims and survivors of pathological relationship abuse recover from the emotional devastation and hurt that inevitably results from a traumatic bond with a disordered personality. But as is often the case, what we encounter on our journey of discovery—both professionally and personally—can lead us to abandon the path we're on for one even more worthwhile. This is what happened with me.

My interest in writing extensively about surviving pathological relationship abuse arose from my own real life horror story, a story of survival and recovery from an intimate relationship with a severely personality disordered partner. Not even my extensive background in the study of psychology and human behavior rendered me immune from inadvertently forging a bond with such a personality.

At the time, I was baffled that I had become so easily ensnared. My bewilderment forced me to come to terms with the reality that I had to let go of much of what I had been formally taught in advanced degree programs, and what I had always believed about human nature and behavior. Moreover, I had to accept the disturbing reality that there are a significant number of human beings who do really horrible things to really good people on purpose. Even more disturbing was the discovery that these disordered individuals do not do horrible things to good people because they were mistreated themselves or because something bad happened to them. Rather, these "do-bad" people consciously and deliberately look for "victims" and seek out opportunities to do horrible things to others *because they can and because they want to.* In fact, science has proven that it's in their very nature to do so.[1]

---

1 Joel Paris, *Myths of Trauma: Why Adversity Does Not Necessarily Make Us Sick* (Oxford University Press, 2023).; Kevin J. Mitchell, *Innate: How the Wiring of Our Brains Shapes Who We Are* (Princeton University Press, 2018).; Robert Plomin, *Blueprint: How DNA Makes Us Who We Are,* (MIT Press, 2019).

Unfortunately, many victims may not realize they are being abused for a very long time. I can attest to this firsthand. If you're reading this book, I think it's safe to assume that you have endured—or may currently be enduring—the same kind of devastation and hurt at the hands of a disordered individual that I experienced. The kind of devastation and hurt that can hijack your entire life. The kind of injury to the psyche that can have you questioning everything you thought you knew about yourself. The kind of agonizing bewilderment that steals your self-respect, your self-esteem, your self-worth, and your self-confidence.

If you are or have been faced with the unfortunate circumstance of being trapped in a relationship with a disordered personality, like a narcissist, a psychopath, a severe borderline personality, or any other type of relational parasite or predator, this book will help you free yourself from the abuse once and for all. However, be forewarned, the kind of trauma that comes from pathological relationship abuse does not heal on its own or with the passage of time.

Though this sounds dire, knowledge is how you fight back. Knowledge can be an extended hand to grasp which will assist you in climbing out of the black hole you were sucked into without even realizing it. This book is designed to help you recover from the type of manipulation, coercion, and abuse that is consciously and deliberately inflicted by pathological individuals that are clinically referred to as personality disordered.

If you let it, this book can be your life saver.

SECTION 1

Recognition

Chapter One

Introduction

Wolves in Sheep's Clothing

Disordered personalities blend in with the crowd. They look, walk, and talk like everybody else, but their relational intentions are not like everyone else's. They exploit, manipulate, and violate other people because they believe they are entitled to do so. These individuals are not as rare as you might think; in fact, a significant percentage of the general human population meets the diagnostic criteria for a severe personality disorder.[2]

Rather than standing out in the crowd, these individuals are expertly camouflaged within it. This is why it's so difficult to distinguish people with good intentions from people with not so

[2] Alan Godwin and Gregory W. Lester, *Demystifying Personality Disorders: Clinical Skills for Working with Drama and Manipulation* (PESI Publishing, 2021).

good intentions. Disordered personalities don't resemble the make-believe monsters underneath our beds or the distinctly ghastly characters we've grown accustomed to seeing in horror films. When you encounter them, they are more likely to be smiling pleasantly rather than snarling or gnashing their teeth. Disordered personalities resemble you, me, and everyone else.

In clinical literature, personality disorders are referred to as "cluster disorders" because some personality disorders have overlapping features, and the majority of individuals who meet the criteria for one personality disorder will also meet the criteria for another disorder or come very close to it.[3] Because the features of personality disorders tend to frequently overlap, it's often exceedingly difficult for victims and survivors to know exactly what kind of person they are dealing with. This is true even if you've been married to a disordered personality for decades, especially when you are caught in a

---

3 Sabine C. Herpertz & Katja Bertsch, "Neuroscience and Personality Disorders," in Personality Disorders and Pathology: Integrating Clinical Assessment and Practice in the DSM-5 and ICD-11 Era, ed. Steven K. Huprich. (American Psychological Association, 2022), 323-349.

web of chronic intentional emotional abuse and truth manipulation.

Traumatic Cognitive Dissonance (TCD)

When truth manipulation and other forms of deceit and coercion are experienced on a chronic basis, the result is a devastating, disorienting, and bewildering form of trauma with a very unique indicator that goes far beyond typical trauma and stress-related symptoms. To describe this unique symptom indicator, I have coined the term Traumatic Cognitive Dissonance (TCD).

Cognitive Dissonance is simply when what you believe doesn't align with what you are experiencing, with reality, or even with your own actions. *Cognitive* refers to thinking while *dissonance* refers to tension or a clash, so cognitive dissonance in simplistic terms is an internal clash within one's thought process. Disconcerting at the very least; paralyzing at worst.

Traumatic Cognitive Dissonance (TCD) can be defined as a distinct form of internal conflict that is the direct result of truth manipulation and covert abuse within the context of a relationship with a disordered personality where the abuser disorients the victim's brain and nervous system with relentless contradictions. This results in contradictory beliefs about yourself, contradictory beliefs about your pathological partner, and contradictory beliefs about the true nature of the relationship dynamic.

In addition to the dissonant thoughts, feelings, and beliefs that constantly intrude upon victims and survivors, traumatic cognitive dissonance simultaneously activates and maintains what is known as dorsal vagal shutdown, which is the "freeze" response in your autonomic nervous system. What begins as intrusive contradictory thoughts becomes a constant state of imbalance. This can be both confusing and demoralizing.

As if all this isn't bad enough, most victims blame *themselves* for thinking and feeling "conflicted" and punish themselves with harsh criticism for not being able to decipher the truth or to just "get over it."[4]

What TCD Feels Like

Here are some examples of how victims and survivors of pathological relationship abuse

---

[4] Sandra. L. Brown, Claudia Paradise, & Bill Brennan, *Intensive Training on Narcissistic and Psychopathic Abuse* (PESI Publishing, 2021).

have described their experience of traumatic cognitive dissonance when consulting with me professionally. Notice how in virtually every case the victim, while still disoriented by the fog of confusion left in their abuser's wake, defaults to blaming themselves.

> "It's been a little over five years since my divorce was finalized, but that didn't really finalize anything. I still don't know whether I was the problem or not. I'm driving myself crazy trying to figure it out. My mind won't stop racing about it. It won't shut off. It's debilitating."

> "I feel the constant need to retaliate, to prove something. But that's never been me. How do I get my family and friends to believe me? To believe what happened to me? Maybe I'm not remembering correctly. My ex often told me that I exaggerate or that I'm overly sensitive. Maybe that's my problem. I was always too sensitive."

"I feel paralyzed. Trapped. I can't move. I can't even do mundane or trivial things anymore. I feel so weak. So helpless. So pathetic."

"Why would any normal person still want to be with someone who treated them so badly? How is it possible that I miss my abuser? I wonder if I'm the one with the disorder. Maybe I'm the narcissist or the borderline. Normal people wouldn't long for an abusive person, would they?"

"I get so angry when they deny everything in light of hard evidence. And yet I still doubt the evidence. I doubt myself. Maybe I'm wrong."

"Why do I want so badly for my ex-partner to know that I'm doing okay, even though I'm not okay. I'm not okay at all. Why can't I just get over this? How do I get to where I don't care what they think?"

"How could he love his ex-wife so much for so long and just discard me so quickly? It must be me. I wish I didn't think that way, but what else could it be?"

"They find holes in everything I say to make me doubt myself, and I can't stand up for myself any longer. I'm frozen in defeat."

"He doesn't even need to try to manipulate me anymore. At this point, I rationalize his deceit all on my own, in my own mind. Maybe I've deceived myself into thinking he's the problem. Maybe I've been the problem all this time. I feel like I did something wrong every second of the day."

"There is a constant pain of 'nowhere to go' in this relationship. I have to go, but I have to stay. I don't know how to do what I have to do. I don't know how to even know what I have to do."

> I constantly fear being discarded and left, while simultaneously knowing full well that it has already happened. That it's coming. But it's already past. How is that possible? I must be going crazy.
>
> "I have so many vengeful thoughts, revenge fantasies, and I've never been a vengeful person. I feel like I'm violating my own morals and values. A good person wouldn't desire revenge."
>
> "Nobody believes me about him/her. It must be me."
>
> "The pain of realizing they don't care, and never cared... that I was tricked."
>
> "My partner is in control of my self-control, and my nervous system hates me."

As you can see in the cases above, the people who suffer from traumatic cognitive dissonance have tried their best and were well-intentioned in their relationships. Becoming involved with a predatory disordered personality was not their fault, because identifying their partner as such early on would have been next to impossible. Then, once fully enmeshed in the relationship, traumatic cognitive dissonance caused them to believe what is not true while simultaneously causing them to be unable to believe what is true while simultaneously causing them to blame themselves for not knowing what is true. To put it simply, traumatic cognitive dissonance is *crazy making*.

How TCD Differs from PTSD

The type of trauma that is experienced within the context of pathological relationship abuse goes far beyond "typical" symptoms of PTSD (Post Traumatic Stress Disorder) and other stressor-related conditions. This is because the truth manipulation tactics that are utilized by social and relational predators in the context of these relationships are very similar to the brainwashing, programming, entrancing, conditioning, and grooming tactics used by pedophiles, cults, and authoritarian institutions.

Because of this, even the most positive and enjoyable moments and memories experienced by victims and survivors in a pathological abuse relationship are traumatizing when they are occurring and retraumatizing when they are being recalled in the present.[5] This strengthens the trauma bond even more regardless of the passage of time or physical proximity.

---

5 Sandra. L. Brown, Claudia Paradise, & Bill Brennan, *Intensive Training on Narcissistic and Psychopathic Abuse* (PESI Publishing, 2021).

Chapter Two

This Book and You

Let Me Introduce Myself

My name is Dr. Peter Salerno, and I am a licensed psychotherapist, clinical supervisor, clinical consultant, trauma-informed educator, and author of seven books, including this one. I specialize in treating trauma that is caused by chronic manipulation at the hands of pathological personalities, specifically Cluster B personalities.

It is my honor to support victims and survivors of this unique and sadly commonly unrecognized and misinterpreted form of abuse while they are on their journey toward understanding, survival, recovery, and healing. My ardent desire is to help victims and survivors of pathological relationship abuse reclaim their personal power and get their lives back.

One of the main reasons I am so passionate about helping and supporting people in this particular way is because I have survived it myself. There is hope. There is recovery. There is life after this form of abuse. And you can do it. You can get your life back, just like I did.

The Difficulty in Finding Professional Help and Support

If you have tried to seek help in the past from a professional to try to make sense of what you've been through, and the professional you sought out was not aware of the distinct form of trauma that results from pathological relationship abuse, it's very likely you found yourself still floundering and searching for some explanation as to why you feel the way you do. We expect professionals not only to be supportive but also to provide enough insight so that a sufferer can make positive changes in their lives. To provide support that would actually help with healing and recovery.

Maybe you had no choice but to become an expert yourself in pathological relationship abuse by doing your own research. It's not fair for victims and survivors to have to do this, but it is very common for those who have not found the help they've needed to become investigative researchers in order to try to make sense of their distinct relational trauma, especially after professional help has failed to do so.

Unfortunately, many professionals inadvertently cause harm to victims and survivors of pathological relationship abuse because they are not properly informed and educated about personality pathology.[6] Because of this, it is all too common to end up with a well-meaning professional who cannot adequately educate you on the true nature of pathological relationship abuse, of the kind of relationship you are actually in, or of the kind of person you are truly dealing with. Without this foundational knowledge, the professional cannot intervene in ways that produce much relief or any lasting recovery. Because of this, the field of mental health has historically let victims and survivors of pathological relationship abuse down. Mental healthcare has not sufficiently validated survivors or helped them recover from their abuse and resulting trauma.

---

6 Alan Godwin and Gregory W. Lester, *Demystifying Personality Disorders: Clinical Skills for Working with Drama and Manipulation* (PESI Publishing, 2021).

One reason is that many mental health professionals don't focus on the impact of personality pathology on relationships. Too many believe that all forms of abuse and relationship dysfunction are the result of the abuser's own developmental trauma or neglect from their childhood.[7] These biases related to childhood adversity theories that mental health professionals hold about disordered personalities have caused immeasurable harm to those who are victimized by them. If a professional believes that all human beings are basically the same on the inside, and they assume that disordered personalities can be reasoned with and for the most part are genuinely willing to collaborate and problem-solve, there is a high likelihood that a victim's experiences will be invalidated. Instead of being fully supported, the victim may be told to "work on the relationship" with a dangerous predator, or worse, told that their own "attachment issues" or "unresolved childhood wounds" are the root cause of the dysfunction

---

7 Carol Tavris, "The Scientist-Practitioner Gap: Revisiting 'A View from the Bridge' a Decade Later," in The Science and Pseudoscience of Clinical Psychology, ed. Scott O. Lilienfeld, Steven J. Lynn, and Jeffrey M. Lohr, 2nd ed. (The Guilford Press, 2015), ix-xx.

in the relationship. Sadly, I've heard variations of these accounts from clients more times than I can count.

When seeking support for pathological relationship abuse, here are some red flags to look for when meeting with a mental health professional:

- They hint or admit they do not "believe" that personality disorders exist as a distinct classification of disorders and instead conceptualize these disorders as environmentally learned behaviors with treatable and even curable symptoms.
- They admit to viewing personality pathology as originating from deep-seated fears or defenses related to inferiority, low self-esteem, and other insecurities.
- They inadvertently sympathize with your abuser for what *they* must have been through to get to the point where they were compelled to mistreat you so badly.
- They interpret the behavior of a pathological personality as resulting from complex trauma and believe personality disorders are caused by adverse childhood experiences and therefore should be

managed with traditional, history-oriented interventions.

Though these mental health professionals may be well-meaning, this ill-informed therapeutic approach has them aligning—at least at first—with the abuser rather than with the victim and survivor. Nothing can be more demoralizing to someone desperately seeking support and validation for what they've gone through than to be asked to not only be intellectually objective but to also empathize with an abuser.

My Unique Approach

This is where my personal experience and professional effectiveness may prove very helpful for the reader of this book. My views on personality pathology, which are based on hard scientific data, differ significantly from the vast majority of professionals in the field of mental health. It is my belief that one of the greatest failures in all of mental health science has been the widespread mis-education about the root cause of personality pathology. Though an in-depth explanation on the etiology or cause of personality disorders is beyond the scope and purpose of this book, this is extensively researched and explained in my book *The Nature and Nurture of Narcissism* for those who are interested in conclusive scientific findings and empirical data.

The book you are reading was created for victims of pathological relationship abuse so that you have a well-informed and accurate understanding of the psychological injuries you've suffered and endured, but also survived. It's important to remember that if you are reading this right now, you are, in fact, a *survivor*, and no one can take that away from you.

I am going to explain, using science-based, empirical research, why pathological personalities are the way they are, and why it is so hard to see who they are from the outset. For our purposes, let me assure you that the missing piece you have been searching for to make sense of your disorienting, debilitating situation so that you may recover once and for all and reunite with your true sense of self can be found in understanding traumatic cognitive dissonance. And that's what this book is all about.

The Proliferation of Misinformation

Your brain and nervous system require clarity about what you have dealt with, and there is a large body of literature on the subject of disordered personalities. Some of it is accurate, but much of it is misinformation presented as fact by experts with legitimate credentials that are based on classical views and theories that were discredited decades ago.

Other information that is popular, especially throughout social media, is based on personal experiences and presented by media influencers who may have, for one reason or another, chosen not to verify or validate their personal claims with scientific evidence on pathological relationship abuse. Their accounts may be interesting, even illuminating, but these should be regarded as anecdotal rather than as a path forward that you should emulate.

You will find concepts in this book based on neuroscience that are likely new to you, as books on the topic of disordered personalities typically default to social and psychological concepts that can be helpful but, based on my clinical experience, can often fall short. We need more effective interventions for victims and survivors of trauma. I trust that the principles you discover in this book will be a breath of fresh air to your brain and your nervous system. While they differ significantly from the classical and traditional views and interventions you are most likely familiar with, they are based on the most recent, up-to-date neuroscientific explanations of how the brain and nervous system actually work. They are effective interventions, and hopefully they will become utilized more and more by mental health professionals who are advocates for victims and survivors of disordered personality predators.

What This Book Isn't

To be clear: this book is more a guidebook than a workbook. Most workbooks have exercises that don't factor in the reality that after pathological relationship abuse you can't rely on self-help exercises alone to heal and recover. Your nervous system is truly hijacked. As long as this is the case you cannot break free from the torment that makes it nearly impossible for you to be able to think and feel accurately about what happened to you. Even if the relationship is cognitively over for you and even if physical proximity is no longer a factor, you are still stuck in hijack mode through no fault of your own.

Because you need both answers and solutions, this book is short and to the point because I'm not going to waste your time with too many exercises and activities. As you are probably already experiencing physical, mental and emotional fatigue and immobilization, you'll need an immediate "boost up." Once the trauma bond is dissolved and traumatic cognitive dissonance is resolved, then you can feel free to participate in whatever activities that will help you rediscover what's been buried for so long.

I completely understand at both a personal and professional level the insatiable need to absorb as much information as possible on how a relationship like this could have happened to you. These relationships do in fact *happen* to you. You don't just come upon them and then willingly stick around to see if it's going to work out. You've inadvertently stepped in what might be described as emotional quicksand where it seems like the more you struggle to free yourself, the deeper you sink. Blaming yourself for not having identified that treacherous quicksand is simply hindsight-gazing and doesn't help you in the now.

Admittedly, many thinking/caring people, myself included, can't help but go down the intellectual rabbit hole by researching and delving into all forms of media containing information on covert manipulation, narcissistic abuse, psychopathic abuse, dark psychology, etc., to try and find that satisfying "reason" as to why this happened to them. They search for that particular thing about themselves that made them susceptible to an abuser in the first place. They search for that particular bit of insight that, once stumbled upon, will get them "over it" so they can stop ruminating and move on with their lives. They search for the proverbial magic bullet that will aid them in "coming to their senses" about a pathological relationship they feel trapped in and ambivalent about. The psychology behind this motivation is understandable, and an in depth investigation is often a necessary part of the journey for many individuals, but it is not a cure-all, not by a long shot.

I'm not going to extensively highlight all of the overt and covert tactics and strategies disordered personalities use to manipulate and coerce their victims. Not in this book, at least. That information is readily available online and in many other sources. And you don't really need all that right now. If you plan on starting a career as a profiler, or if you simply find abnormal psychology and behavior fascinating, you can study up to your heart's content. But the accumulation of pure knowledge is not the key to breaking free from traumatic abuse. Having successfully worked with countless survivors of pathological relationship abuse, I have found that descriptive pathology only gets them so far. It's the explanatory pathology that needs to be understood.

What This Book Is

I've been where you are now, and I can tell you that there *is* hope. There is an end to your suffering in sight. Your dignity, self-esteem, and your ability to trust others can and will be restored. You will be able to move on to healthy relationships and be free to find the relationship you long for and deserve. For some of you, this is also your story, and your future. If you are now or have been a victim, this is where your abuse ends.

This book will teach you to recognize predatory behavior such as covert and overt abuse and manipulation and help you to remove yourself from these relationships while also teaching you how to avoid relational predators in the future. You will learn how to identify the disturbing and often dangerous signs that you are being manipulated by a relational predator. This book will dissolve misguided notions that you are the problem or that it "always takes two." You're not. It doesn't. This book is intended to be a roadmap to freedom, stability, and safety.

The Importance of Accepting the Truth

I am going to briefly highlight the "must know" features of personality pathology that dramatic, erratic, dangerous, and severe personalities have in common that are predictors of abusiveness for those who are in relationships with them. But *why* people are disordered is exceedingly more difficult for victims to wrap their minds around than *what* a disordered person is like to deal with. The *what* is something that is experienced; the *why* is much more elusive.

The bottom line is this, if you don't understand and accept the actual *why*—the true motive of your abuser—you might hold onto false hope that the disordered person you are dealing with will one day change. This false hope will keep you stuck in non-recovery mode and mired deep in the trenches of traumatic cognitive dissonance.

If, on the rare occasion, a disordered personality decides they do want to try to change some things about their personality, these changes are not going to occur because you stuck around. It is not your presence *or* absence in their lives that is going to serve as the motivation for change or as an agent of change. The path to change for some less severely disordered personalities, when change is possible, must be left up to professionals who know how to work with their kind of personality structure. This, quite honestly, is not your problem to deal with, and making it your problem is too costly in too many ways.

Continuing Your Journey

Don't be concerned if there are times when you feel confused, overwhelmed, stuck, or fearful when reading this book. Such feelings are completely natural when revisiting the traumatic aspects of pathological relationship abuse. Just keep going and know that this book is designed to inform, clarify, and ultimately create a path to recovery that will actually work. Once your recovery path is established, you can then seek professional help using this book as a primer and manual for the specific help you'll need.

There is support out there, and I will explain how to find the right kind of help later on. After years of working with countless victims and survivors of pathological relationship abuse, I can suggest the most effective interventions for dismantling trauma bonds and resolving traumatic cognitive dissonance and I will make recommendations for this as well.

How This Book Is Organized

This book is divided into three sections. The first section (Recognition) explores how to recognize the signs that indicate you may be suffering from traumatic cognitive dissonance and did not even know it, or if you did know it but didn't know what to call it. Either way, you didn't have any idea what to do about it. And maybe neither does your current therapist nor did the previous mental health professionals you desperately sought answers from.

The second section (Identification) will assist you in identifying how traumatic cognitive dissonance presents itself in your life. It will also describe what happens to your brain and nervous system when subjected to chronic manipulation and abuse on the part of a disordered personality, and how it has truly impacted you. This section will also provide what I refer to as the Social Predator's Secret Playbook, which is a list of the most common manipulation tactics used by disordered personalities. These manipulation tactics, as you might guess, are things social predators don't want their victims or would-be victims knowing anything about.

The third section (Recovery) will introduce you to healing techniques and exercises that are designed to help you rediscover and reunite with your true sense of self, the person you know yourself to be, the good person buried underneath all the truth manipulation, coercion, subterfuge, and the other forms of abuse you've been subjected to. Your core self—despite whatever you've gone through—is certainly not gone for good and has not been permanently damaged. No matter what has happened or what you believe about yourself right now, who you really are is still inside like a dormant flowering plant.

Also in this section is information on the most effective trauma interventions should you decide (and I highly recommend you do) to seek additional support from a professional who understands pathological relationship abuse and knows how to successfully alleviate the symptoms of traumatic cognitive dissonance.

Proceed Mindfully and Self-Caringly

This content may be emotionally activating at times. Respectfully, that is not a reason not to press forward. Trust your resiliency. You've already survived hell. You can survive taking care of yourself. Do not allow your abuser to have power over your healing process. This book is for you, not them. They may have put you through hell, but they cannot keep you there unless you let them. I don't mean to sound harsh. But I had to teach myself this lesson, and I truly wish I would have had someone to offer practical solutions when I was digging myself out of the trenches of abuse and manipulation. I wish someone would have woken me up much sooner. Not that I would have listened or gone willingly, at least not at first, but if I'd known the truth about these personalities back when, and had known that holding onto hope was futile, I would have done things differently, even though it still would have been extremely difficult. It would have saved me some valuable time and valuable and sentimental resources I had to let go of in order to survive.

Because I've been where you are now, this book was written to push you. So get ready. I have faith in you. Have faith in yourself.

That being said, it is more than okay to take breaks when going through this book, and it's also okay to pace yourself. Put the book down if and when you feel the need to and come back to it when you're ready. But whatever you do, don't give up. Doing so will be giving your power away. I guarantee if your story is anything like mine, you were manipulated, coerced, and forced into giving up your power and agency in countless ways while you were being victimized. Even if the relationship has ended, you may still feel just as powerless at times. This is exactly why you need to honor yourself by doing whatever it takes to reclaim your personal foundation, to rediscover yourself, and to move toward thriving with confidence and a sense of peace.

SECTION 2

Identification

Chapter Three

Pulling Back the Curtain on Disordered Personalities

So What Are Disordered Personalities?

Most of us were taught to believe that all human beings think and feel in similar ways. Specifically, that for the most part, everyone thinks and feels in the same ways that *we* do. This isn't always the case, and unfortunately, it is quite dangerous to go through life thinking it is. Contrary to popular belief, there are people who are born with genetic and neurobiological deficits and impairments in personality structure and function.[8] We call these individuals Disordered Personalities because personality disorders, unlike other mental

8 Kevin J. Mitchell, *Innate: How the Wiring of Our Brains Shapes Who We Are* (Princeton University Press, 2018).

disorders, are disorders of the entire person—of the entire structure of the self. Think of it this way: a Disordered Personality's entire operating system is misaligned and for the most part not repairable in any meaningful way.

A Disordered Personality's disordered traits are not "learned behaviors" or "symptoms" or "episodes," nor are they unresolved attachment issues or inner child wounds.[9] It is not what *happened* to these people that makes them think, feel, and behave the way they do, although they tend to thrive and their pathology will metastasize if you believe they were once victims themselves. They are the way they are because they were wired that way from the beginning.[10]

In fact, there are actually empty spaces and missing pieces in the brain structure of disordered personalities. This is one of the most challenging and disturbing realities for decent people to wrap their heads around. However, accepting this reality as a given is what you are going to need to do in order to heal and recover from

---

9 Alan Godwin and Gregory W. Lester, *Demystifying Personality Disorders: Clinical Skills for Working with Drama and Manipulation* (PESI Publishing, 2021).

10 Robert Plomin, Blueprint: How DNA Makes Us Who We Are, (MIT Press, 2019).

pathological relationship abuse and resolve your traumatic cognitive dissonance. Since they can't change who they are, it's up to you to change how you regard them.

There are many differences between how personality disordered people and neurotypical (normal) people think, feel, believe, perceive, relate, and behave. For starters, the trait of empathy is severely impaired or altogether missing from the brains of most severely disordered personalities. This is a point that is extremely difficult for victims, or really for anyone with empathy capability, to fully grasp and accept. Most disordered personalities simply do not possess the neurological capacity to care about your feelings. These disordered personalities are self-absorbed pathological liars who consistently and incessantly manipulate others. They do not experience guilt or remorse after they hurt others, and this is why they can physically and emotionally injure those they profess to love without a tinge of regret or concern for the suffering of their victims. Their thinking, feeling, and behavioral processes are not just different: they are *disordered.*

Disordered personalities are missing pieces of "self" that most people mistakenly believe are inherent in everyone, and many of these disordered individuals behave in ways that could almost convince us they are a separate or subhuman species. I want to stress this: their entire operating system is different from neurotypical individuals like yourself. Because of their complete lack of sincerity, interacting with a disordered personality is tantamount to interacting with a fictional character. Even if you have known a disordered personality for years, you really don't know anything about them. And they don't know much about themselves either because there really is no "self" to get to know.

These manipulators are incapable of developing a fully integrated identity and sense of self. They are fragmented creatures at best, collecting scraps of identity, Frankenstein monster-style, from people they victimize as well as from people they choose to emulate. Because they have a predator's ability to tilt reality in their favor, they have a distinct advantage over others. And once they hook you into their drama, they can actually end up knowing you better than you know yourself.

Intimacy with a disordered personality is not all that intimate because disordered personalities have severe impairments when it comes to interpersonal relationships. This includes a refusal on their end to be held accountable for their participation in relational conflicts. Because they have an inherent lack of interest in collaborating with anyone, they display an unwillingness to cooperate even at the most basic level in relationships all while feigning earnest collaboration and cooperation.

The Compensation Myth

Unfortunately, common but discredited knowledge continues to permeate academia and research on disordered personalities. One such prevailing falsehood is that people who commit truth manipulation are doing so as a result of some sense of inferiority or inadequacy stemming from childhood. We can thank pop psychology culture and errors in research for this disaster of inaccuracy.

While childhood abuse and neglect are risk factors of trauma in individuals with neurotypical brains, and while many pathological personalities were in fact treated badly early in life, the disordered personalities who either were or still are wreaking havoc in your life are not suffering from inferiority complexes or deep-seated fears and insecurities. This is a common misconception. They are *not* emotionally defending themselves against anything from their past or present; they are simply playing offense.

Relational predators and parasites are not *reacting* out of a fear-based threat response; they are *acting* out of a desire-based intimidation response. They hurt others when they don't get exactly what they want. This is offense, not defense. When they don't get what they want, their switch flips. But it's not a self-esteem switch. It's a temper tantrum switch. Their aggressive and devious behaviors are not the result of any underlying fear. Instead, their behaviors are deliberate and are carried out with malice, cruelty, and even—for some—great delight.

It is important to keep reminding yourself as you go through your journey of recovery that, when applied to pathological relationship abuse, the most traditional psychological theories are categorically flawed. For one thing, these theories have historically been based on anecdotal information coming from the abusers themselves. Because of this, effective or even reasonably sufficient results in clinical treatment with disordered personalities are seldom obtained. In short, the prevailing notion that disordered personalities behave badly because they feel bad about their childhoods doesn't hold up.

Disordered Personalities Checklist

The following is a list of traits, characteristics and behaviors of disordered personalities. Though these personalities may not overtly exhibit every item on the list, most will embody quite a few.

- They lash out overtly *and* covertly when disagreed with
- They are impulsive
- They externalize their internal distress so that others experience it
- They refuse and don't intend to collaborate
- They use others for their own one-sided purposes
- They don't admit to their part in creating problems
- They are controlling, combative, entitled, coercive, manipulative, and inconsiderate toward others (*pathologically narcissistic*, in other words).

- They use emotional blackmail, even literal blackmail, and threats
- They have a high potential for violence toward themselves and others
- They deny responsibility
- They have a high rate of substance abuse
- Their core functioning vacillates between trait deficiency and excess
- They misrepresent the truth through lying and distorting reality
- They do not respond to traditional symptom-oriented psychotherapy
- They are in fact sane, but their disordered functioning makes it seem like they must be crazy.
- The disordered "language" they speak creates drama rather than solves problems.[11]

Disordered Personality Traits

A personality trait is a propensity to think, feel, perceive, believe, and behave in relatively consistent ways. It is important to distinguish traits from symptoms because symptoms ebb and

---

[11] Alan Godwin and Gregory W. Lester, *Demystifying Personality Disorders: Clinical Skills for Working with Drama and Manipulation* (PESI Publishing, 2021).

flow, whereas traits are more stable. Personality traits are characteristic rather than symptomatic. It is also important to note that personality traits, like physical traits, are heritable, so they are much different from learned behaviors or symptoms acquired due to life experiences.

Cluster B personalities include Borderline, Antisocial, Narcissistic, and Histrionic Personality Disorders. There are a number of identifiable pathological personality traits common to Cluster B personalities that might very well, in their descriptions below, sound familiar to you in terms of your experience with the disordered personality or personalities in your life.

> **Emotional lability.** Unstable moods; unstable emotional experiences; easily aroused emotions; intense and rapid emotional shifts that are out of proportion to most contexts and circumstances.

> **Hostility.** Persistent contempt; irritable; prone to anger or rage in response to perception of even minor slights; cruel and vengeful; spiteful and sadistic.

Perseveration: Insistence on doing things a certain way; continuing to do things in a certain way even after that way has proven to be ineffective; persisting in the same behaviors despite repeated consequences and obvious reasons for stopping that behavior.

Antagonism Intentionally oppositional; behaving in ways that force people to be at odds with one another. Maintaining interpersonal problems by being domineering, self-serving, and vindictive.

Manipulativeness. Taking advantage of and exploiting others through lying, deceiving, and cheating. Employing subterfuge and coercion to influence and control other people; presenting oneself in deceptive, seductive, charming, and superficial ways to fulfill one's own distorted purposes. Behaving in overtly and covertly dishonest ways.

Deceitfulness. Creating false and misleading impressions; misrepresenting oneself; exaggerating or creating false accounts of events and circumstances; persistently dishonest and duplicitous.

Dominance. A need for power that results in being controlling, authoritarian, and forceful in interpersonal interactions.

Grandiosity. Arrogance and entitlement. Believing that one is superior to others and deserving of special treatment; self-centeredness; condescension toward others; an exaggerated sense of self-importance and a disbelief in equality.

Attention Seeking. Constantly attempting to make oneself the primary focus of attention and admiration regardless of circumstances.

Callousness. Cold-heartedness; mean spiritedness; lack of interest and concern for the rights, feelings, and wellbeing of others; lack of guilt or remorse related to harmful effects of one's actions and their impact on others.

Exhibitionism. Engaging in and deriving pleasure from overt attention-seeking behaviors; behaving in an overly showy and theatrical manner that includes exaggerated spectacles of emotion; behaving and presenting in highly sexual and provocative ways.

Rudeness. Interpersonal insensitivity; blunt and tactless interpersonal communication.

Social Norm Violation. Rejection of social rules and agreements; engaging in illegal, antisocial, and rebellious actions; disobedient and defiant behavior.

Gratification-seeking. Orientation toward immediate gratification, leading to impulsive behavior driven by current thoughts, feelings, and external stimuli, without regard for past learning or consideration of future consequences.

Irresponsibility. Blatant disregard for and refusal to honor important, agreed-upon obligations or commitments; disdain for agreements and promises; carelessness.

Impulsivity. Acting without a plan or concern for potential consequences.

Risk Taking. Engaging in activities purely because they are stimulating, exhilarating, and potentially dangerous without concern for one's limitations and denial of the reality of potential danger; reckless pursuit regardless of risk.

Restricted Affect. Little reaction to emotionally arousing situations; constricted emotional experience and expression; indifference to socially engaging situations.[12]

12 Whitney R. Ringwald et al., "Structure of Pathological Personality Traits Through the Lens of the CAT-PD Model," *Assessment*, (2023): 30, no.7, 2276-2295.

Chapter Four

Where You Come into the Picture

The Complexity of Emotional Experience

Keep in mind, people differ tremendously in their ability to accurately describe their emotional experiences and they differ in how accurately they are able to read their internal emotional states when experiencing Traumatic Cognitive Dissonance. Studies have shown that many individuals use words like "sad," "afraid," "anxious," and "depressed" interchangeably to mean the same thing or to refer to a general feeling of unpleasantness or discomfort.[13]

While suffering from Traumatic Cognitive Dissonance, many individuals may have difficulty

13 Lisa Feldman Barrett, *How Emotions Are Made: The Secret Life of the Brain* (Harper, 2018).

detecting physical cues or reactions to their emotions and interpreting them accurately. What's important is that you learn to identify and describe exactly what *you* feel and not rely on some generic definition. You are complex and so are your feelings, but, with a little work, you can find the most accurate label for them.

What You May Be Experiencing

Symptoms of Traumatic Cognitive Dissonance develop both during and after relationships with disordered personalities. In fact, there is strong empirical evidence that individuals who develop trauma-related conditions during and following a relationship with a disordered personality experience significant disruptions in their core belief system.

These disrupted beliefs are manifested in inaccurate self-statements that interrupt or pause the normal recovery process.[14] Beliefs that are disrupted or that are installed by coercion and truth manipulation on the part of a disordered personality are often shame-based. Disrupted

---

14 Patricia A. Resick, Candice M. Monson, and Kathleen M. Chard, Cognitive Processing Therapy for PTSD: A Comprehensive Manual (The Guilford Press, 2017).

beliefs can also be related to a sense of lack of safety and lack of control, and to assuming responsibility for what is not one's fault. Due to the nature, structure and functioning of personality disordered brains, being on the receiving end of such abuse can be brutal and unrelenting.

Here are some of the most common indicators that traumatic cognitive dissonance may be occurring within you:

- Rumination or "racing thoughts" about the relationship make you feel "amped up" and "shut down" at the same time.
- Loss of cognitive control of your behavior and possibly acting out of character as a result (diminished executive functioning).
- Discursive thoughts, feelings, and beliefs related to self-identity (as if you don't know who you are anymore).
- Emotional paralysis/feeling stuck/chronic "freeze" response.
- Heightened defensiveness and sensitivity/inability to detect a genuine threat of safety from a perceived one, and fearing both.
- Complete loss of self-worth.

- Excessive self-blame.
- Dissociative experiences like staring into space/tuning out/losing time.
- Random reassembling of memories of your abusive relationship which confuse you and cause you to question how you truly feel about your abuser. This can also cause you to question whether you are even capable of accurately grasping the relationship dynamics or if you have made the right decision about the status of the relationship (staying or leaving).
- Unwarranted feelings of extreme guilt and shame.
- The feeling or fear that you have "gone crazy" and you cannot trust yourself, your perception, or your own judgment.
- A profound sense of emotional isolation.
- Desire for physical isolation while simultaneously needing to be with others so as to be supported and understood.
- Inability to make even the most basic, trivial, everyday decisions.
- Pushing away your instincts and intuition.
- Experiencing constant fear and threat states without an identifiable cause.

- Thought immobilization. Feeling stuck in the same thought without being able to stay focused enough to make a decision or come to any conclusions.
- Difficulty processing communication with others or engaging in dialogue.
- Insomnia or hypersomnia. Or both.
- Psychomotor immobilization (difficulty physically functioning and getting your body to move at will).
- Feeling like a fraud or a failure.
- Feeling like an imposter.
- Terrifying vivid nightmares or vivid images throughout the day that come seemingly out of nowhere.
- Worst case scenario thoughts.
- Inability to disengage from your former partner in a variety of ways, e.g. looking up their social media accounts, going over past conversations and arguments, arguing "with them" internally to try and prove points that they dismissed even after you are no longer in contact with them.
- Generalized anxiety.
- Hypervigilance.
- Inability to create a personal sense of safety.

- Suicidal ideation resulting from emotional and physical fatigue rather than from depression or self-loathing.

Even if you are only experiencing a few of these symptoms on the traumatic cognitive dissonance checklist, your sense of wellbeing can be significantly disrupted. Existing in this disruptive mental state can be confusing, demoralizing and ultimately very stressful.

Feeling Frozen in Place

In addition to the random dissonant thoughts, feelings, and beliefs that relentlessly intrude upon a victim of pathological relationship abuse, traumatic cognitive dissonance also simultaneously activates and maintains a chronic "freeze" response in the autonomic nervous system. The brain of a victim assembles multiple neural pathways of fear, shame, and doubt that activate reminders of the abuse and maintain cognitive dissonance. This happens as a result of sustained manipulation and abuse from a disordered personality. These reminders of your trauma and manipulation sustain your dissonant beliefs about yourself, others, and the world around you.

Here's how it works: whenever we perceive danger, social engagement is instinctively the first thing we seek out. If we succeed in finding a safe person during a threat response, relaxation occurs; if we can't find someone to co-regulate with and feel safe with when we're in danger, fight or flight is instinctively activated. If fight or flight is prevented or is not an option, freezing occurs.[15] It is this freeze response that becomes the baseline level of functioning for individuals who are suffering from traumatic cognitive dissonance as a result of pathological relationship abuse.

The dorsal vagal complex or freeze response system is the oldest threat response system in the body.[16] While the dorsal vagal state is designed to promote survival, prolonged activation of this "freeze state" as a result of chronic fear can lead to the mental haziness and physiological stress

---

15 J. Eric Gentry, Forward-Facing Freedom: Healing the Past, Transforming the Present, a Future on Purpose. Parker, CO: Outskirts Press (2021).

16 J. Eric Gentry, Forward-Facing Freedom: Healing the Past, Transforming the Present, a Future on Purpose. Parker, CO: Outskirts Press (2021).

that are characteristic of traumatic cognitive dissonance. Dorsal vagal "shutdown" puts the mind and body into a paralysis of sorts. Not only is this chronic immobilization physically and emotionally exhausting, but it's also disorienting and confusing for the victim. It's as if you can't figure out what's wrong while at the same time you can't figure out why you can't figure it out.

Traumatic cognitive dissonance is one of the most debilitating trauma symptoms that can occur after being involved with a disordered personality. Unfortunately, it is also almost completely undetected, overlooked, misunderstood, or surprisingly, even denied by the vast majority of mental health professionals who specialize in treating complex trauma.

Conflicting Emotions

You may experience conflicting emotions that cause you to believe that you must remain loyal to your pathological partner. You may feel guilty, selfish, disloyal, or unloving for talking about them to a professional. But this is a trick your mind plays on you after chronic manipulation.

You may fear that *you* are actually the pathological one and have unreasonable expectations in your relationships. You may experience retaliation after setting boundaries with a pathological individual, such as being cut off from family, losing relationships, and being lied about and blamed for the relationship souring. Unfortunately, setting boundaries with a pathological partner may result in many inevitable and unforeseen consequences to your social and emotional life, but only temporarily. Keep in mind, these consequences, no matter how devastating they may feel at first, are not worth the pain of staying in a pathological abuse relationship in order to avoid them.

Why Were You Targeted?

I want to make this abundantly clear: you were <u>not</u> chosen by a disordered personality because you are a born victim. You weren't and you're not. Even if you are highly sensitive, even if you are lacking in self-esteem, even if you are insecurely attached, even if you have been identified as an "empath," or even if a previous professional managed to convince you that you struggle with "codependency," you are not identifiable prey to every predatory personality. In fact, some of these descriptors are so grossly overused and misused that they cause more confusion than clarity, and none of them are recognized as formal diagnoses.

Who *you* are is not the reason you ended up in a relationship with a disordered personality. The shocking truth is this: any decent human being with a pulse and the capacity to love and the desire to be loved in return is susceptible to falling prey to truth manipulation and is vulnerable to being targeted by a disordered personality. You weren't targeted because there is something wrong with you. The fact that they know you exist is all it takes.

I was studying graduate psychology when I was targeted and duped, and over forty percent of the individuals who reach out to me on a regular basis seeking help to resolve traumatic cognitive dissonance hold one or more of the following credentials: MD, PhD, PsyD, DO, JD, LPCC, LMFT, PA, LMHC, Ed.D., etc. You get the point. Suffice it to say, if you too were sucker punched, you're in really good company. Fancy degrees do not make one immune to truth manipulation. Having common sense doesn't make you immune. Being wary doesn't make you immune. The only qualification you need is being alive and being human.

Disordered individuals vet *anyone* to see how much of a psychological beating they can withstand, and they latch onto you when they are satisfied with your tolerance and resiliency. It is <u>not</u> true that disordered personalities prey on the weak. Quite the contrary, they prey on everyone, but they *depend* on the strong.

When you're constantly being told everything is your fault, you may feel the blame rests solely on you. You may even excuse the other person because of things that have supposedly happened to them in their lives. The disordered personality depends on your strength, not your weakness, to carry the blame for their behavior. Most likely you became their apologist, taking on the weighty responsibility of trying to "make nice" in their destructive wake or of trying to shift the blame away from them for the sake of harmony. If you were truly weak, you would have been of no use to them. It's your strength that they seek to co-opt.

Two Steps Forward, One Step Back

A warning is in order. Even with all the drama, the one-sided investment, the conflict, and the uncertainty, those who are in a pathological abuse relationship often don't want to leave despite the fact that they *need* to leave. The biochemical reaction that takes place within them, fortified by psychological manipulation, combines to basically dig a bottomless pit for the victim that becomes familiar in the way any bad relationship becomes familiar. The old saying "the devil you know is better than the devil you don't," sounds amusing but it really suggests stasis is better than growth—it's not.

Interestingly, once some victims of disordered personalities have won their freedom, they report that new relationships and life in general are boring by comparison to their time with the disordered person. But this is just their bodies adjusting to peaceful living without the flood of adrenaline. Their bodies have been conditioned for the adrenaline rush that goes with all the arguments, conflict, and relentless manipulation. But, have faith: it's only a matter of time until that quest for a sustained negative "high" subsides.

Believing and Feeling

You need to become abundantly clear about what you believe is true about yourself, your partner, and the relationship, and what feels true inside your body about yourself, your partner, and the relationship. Thoughts and feelings affix themselves to each other like a molecular bond and form beliefs. Once these beliefs are formed they become your reality, whether they are accurate or not. If thoughts and feelings are incongruent, the beliefs that are created as a result are *dissonant*, thereby keeping you stuck in non-recovery mode.

The relational bond is not based on anyone having power over you after the relationship ends. The bond is sustained by dissonant beliefs resulting from inaccurate and incongruent thoughts and feelings that have become automatic predictions by your brain. Essentially, the wrong information or data is swimming around your nervous system and getting in your way. It's not you; it's your beliefs. And your brain thinks it's doing you a favor by ruminating about this information. You need to convince your brain otherwise.

Emotional pain is the result of experiencing emotions that are accompanied by threat responses activated by our nervous system. The "meanings" we give to our emotional experiences, if left unexamined, can become risk factors for physical illness and unresolved complex trauma.

A First Step: Asking Yourself Painful Questions

The following are some questions for you to ask yourself and to have in mind as you read these pages. Having a baseline understanding of how you feel and what you believe is step one on your journey to healing and recovery. The answers may be painful to face at first but denial is a roadblock to healing and not a viable strategy. Be honest with yourself, and be kind to yourself. Just asking these questions means you've come a long way.

- What would it mean if it were actually true that your partner intentionally hurt you? That you were betrayed? Can you walk toward that reality? Can you lean into it?
- What *do* you believe about yourself because of what your partner did? What *did* you believe about yourself before your partner came into your life?
- Did you deserve what happened to you? The answer to this question is "No" but do you feel and know that the answer is no? Do you feel like you deserved what

happened even though you cognitively understand you didn't?

- What emotions do you experience when it comes to what happened to you or what is still happening to you? Anger? Disgust? Frustration? Sadness? Fear? Anguish?
- What emotional and moral meanings has your brain created around the pathological relationship that in reality don't belong to you? Guilt? Shame? Regret? Responsibility? Defectiveness? Fault? Flaw?

Though facing the questions can be tough, simply acknowledging your answers can put you in the right frame of mind to proceed without overwhelming anxiety or dread about what you *may* uncover about yourself.

Don't Go It Alone

Where disordered personalities tend to be emotional loners, you don't have to be. It is precisely your ability to be open and social that is an anathema to their manipulative behaviors. When you're enmeshed in an abusive environment, it is a good idea to seek out a support group or a competent mental health advocate in addition to self-help resources. Community support groups and professionals who are familiar with personality pathology and pathological relationship abuse can help you discern what's really going on with you, your partner, and the relationship. Getting an objective opinion is especially useful when you are under duress.

If your symptoms are episodic and present *only* when you're with your partner, then the partner and the relationship are likely the root cause of the turmoil. By differentiating between normal functioning and abnormal functioning, a clearer picture of your situation will present itself. You will be able to discern more clearly where the needle rests for you. That is your first objective: to remember who you really are.

No, it won't be easy, but it will be worth the effort.

Chapter Five

Tactics and Tools of the Disordered Personality

Mirroring and Mimicking

It's exceedingly difficult for people to know if they are being manipulated or abused, especially when the abuse and manipulation are covert or concealed by a disordered personality.[17] Disordered personalities use mimicking and mirroring to ensnare their victims and they can mimic and mirror so deceitfully that you can end up bonding with someone who is nothing like you, all while being convinced you have met your soul mate.

---

17 George K. Simon Jr., Character Disturbance: The Phenomenon of Our Age (Parkhurst Brothers Publishers, 2011).

Relationships with disordered personalities are always fraught with deceit, even if it's well hidden at first. Empathy is cleverly mimicked and manipulated by relational predators. We tend to fall for people who seem to be like us, who have suffered in similar ways as we have, and who share our goals. But these personalities are not like us; they are just mirroring our empathy and our sympathy and compassion for others because they have none of their own.

Disordered personalities are not inadvertent predators; they know what they are doing. They zero in on our humanity and intentionally exploit it. Some do it in an opportunistic predatory fashion, and others do it in a more preferential predatory fashion, but the resulting damage is the same.

When you have been effectively mirrored and mimicked by a disordered personality, you unconsciously see yourself in them—your true, good self. Because of this, because you see yourself in the false mirror, when the relationship starts to unravel as discomfort, dread and uncertainty set in, you may wonder if the reason the relationship deteriorated is because you are to blame.

How do you know you aren't the one responsible for all the negativity? Because you have genuine concern that you are the one at fault while your partner claims no responsibility whatsoever. Pathological personalities seldom accept responsibility for anything, especially when it comes to relationships. It's always the other person's fault. If you ask them to help solve a relational issue with you, they rarely if ever work at it because to do so would be admitting they are at least partially to blame.

Disordered personalities work at destabilizing your self-esteem by constantly telling you that your reality is delusional. They deflect the challenges and objections you raise and turn the tables on you. They are very convincing, especially at convincing you that you are to blame. By systematically deconstructing your reality and thought processes, they make sure they are in total control while you feel completely out of control and emotionally destabilized.

Tactical Manipulation

To understand how to free yourself from pathological relationships, it's critical to know the tactics used to keep you imprisoned and how they are employed against you. These tactical behaviors—whether schemes, ploys, or strategies—can be so skillfully covert that they are barely perceptible to you if at all. It is in the best interest of the disordered personality to keep you spinning in the dark and focused on what you most likely have been told—and have come to believe—are *your* shortcomings and flaws.

If you are fixated on your part in the relationship equation rather than your partner's, it will be difficult to see the tactics that are being used to entrap you, but that's the idea. The disordered personality never wants you to know what they are really up to. Therefore, it's critical to identify the tactics that have been employed to bind you to the abuse. Once you are aware of these and can identify what to watch out for, you'll be able to initiate countermeasures that will both protect you and free you.

Lying

At the very core of most manipulation tactics is lying. The brains of pathological personalities and social predators are literally wired for deception. Lies are the inner fibers of their being. They mask their true intentions with a constructed veneer of lies. Lying is second nature to them. They don't view lying as wrong. If you get hurt by their lies, that's your fault, not theirs. It's best to realize at the outset that pathological personalities have no real moral high ground. Yet they count on you being truthful and having a moral high ground because it's easier for them to manipulate you.

Lying for pathological personalities is a way of life. Because they have an innate sense of false entitlement, a relational predator justifies their lying by believing they alone are entitled to do whatever is in their own best interest. They view themselves as above everyone else and, accordingly, will do whatever they please to accomplish their goals, no matter who gets hurt. To attain what they want, they will stop at nothing. It's actually more than a tactic; it's their standard operating procedure.

Pathological personalities have a natural gift for creating compelling tales that further their agenda. Lying about where they've been, the people they were with and what they were doing, is par for the course. Their lies come as easy as breathing to these individuals and they are adept at building metaphoric ramparts to protect their deceptive behaviors. Since they never want you to know what they're doing, they lie about everything.

Disordered personalities tell lies in their personal lives, in their workplace, and in casual social settings. They lie because they can get away with it. While they may not like it when others lie to them, they view themselves as special people for whom lying is a birthright. What can be perplexing to well-meaning neurotypical (normal) people is that disordered personalities even lie when it doesn't matter or isn't even necessary to misrepresent the truth. They may lie when no reason exists for them to do so. Lying is their default position, not an emergency strategy.

Denial

Denial is a specific form of strategic lying. The sort of denial the manipulator uses is not an unconscious defense mechanism; they are fully aware of what they are doing and why. When they deny, they are not defending; they are performing. Denial is a tactic that is used to wear their victim down in order to further control them. Good intentioned people will typically give the manipulator the benefit of the doubt when they deny having done or not done something because they wrongly assume that the person they are dealing with thinks and feels the way they do. Denial is often inserted into a conversation where partners are discussing something that previously took place as a form of gaslighting. When a manipulator says something didn't occur when you are almost certain it did, for example, this can set your mind spinning. You may question your memory or even if you are imagining things. This tactic of abuse is so corrosive that over time the victim can feel chronically depressed, anxious, helpless, and disoriented.

Here's a quick stratagem for coping with traumatic cognitive dissonance and finding balance after too-long a ride on the disordered personality's rollercoaster. Say this to yourself, aloud if you can:

"I must stop assuming the disordered person in my life knows what I mean when I say ______________________________.
When the disordered person in my life says ______________________________,
and I know they will, I have to remember that I ____________________________"

And repeat as needed. It's a temporary fix but it can work, at least for now. The next section is where your recovery can begin rapidly.

SECTION 3

Recovery

Chapter Six

Freeing Yourself from a Disordered Personality

In order to free yourself from your abuser both in your physical world and in your internal world, you must accept that change must occur both within your nervous system and within your core belief system. If you continue to expect reason, problem-solving, collaboration, or any other form of adaptive change to occur in a pathological personality, you will be disappointed. As long as "nourishment" remains free flowing from you to the manipulator, you probably won't be able to free yourself emotionally or physically. It's like being stuck in quicksand; the more you flail, the deeper you sink. It's a vicious cycle.

Unrealistic expectations and wishful thinking need to be replaced with the acceptance that if change was going to occur, it would already have occurred. Even if you do manage to escape the relationship, you most likely will have to deal with post-relationship contact and abuse. You may get a call from them telling you how much they miss and love you and how wrong they were. They'd give anything to get you back. Because we all want to believe that others also experience remorse and have the capacity to grow and change, we strive to be open to pleas of forgiveness and declarations of love. Unfortunately, disordered personalities are incapable of growth and change and our forgiveness of their past transgressions only serves to start the vicious cycle all over again.

Does *No Contact* Actually Work?

Even if you are completely out of the relationship, the nature of a disordered personality will push them to re-engage with you. They crave control and advantage over others and this is not something they can achieve on their own. But if you reengage with them, you'll be right back in the thick of it.

The No Contact technique as a way of cutting off a disordered personality's source of nourishment—much like depriving a vampire of access to your blood supply—can be extremely effective but does not dissolve the bond within your brain and body. No Contact is merely the first step in leaving the relationship. However, be prepared for the side-effects of this. If you're married, expect that your divorce may be complicated, especially if you have children together. Recognizing that there will inevitably be some pretty vile retaliation can help you prepare for what may be a difficult transition.

Brace Yourself for What Comes Next

While you—as a feeling person—may be in a mourning period following the end of a relationship and not interested in seeking another mate too quickly, don't be surprised when the disordered personality enters into a new relationship almost immediately. In fact, in all probability, they were already in another relationship, or a series of relationships, that you never knew about, before your relationship with them even ended. Don't allow this to hurt you but be relieved that much of their malignant attention is no longer focused on you.

Hopefully, their next victim will stumble upon resources to help them, but this cannot be your concern right now, and you cannot make it your business either. Trying to inform others, to protect them, to warn them, or to seek justice before you have recovered and while you are still trauma-bonded will only keep you stuck. It's an ineffectual way of staying connected to your abuser that won't help a new victim and that will not help you.

Focus on the Open Road Ahead, Not on the Wreckage Behind

Keeping your emotions focused on yourself and on healing from abuse from a disordered personality will shield you from any further emotional involvement. If they are not fed—nourished by your well-meaning capitulation—their hold on you will weaken. If you have zero expectations, if you accept that you can't cure or change the relationship for the better, if you admit to yourself that no matter how hard you try you cannot save any other victims from them right now, you will be able to protect yourself from further harm. This is not *giving up*, it's *wising up*.

Remember this: disordered personalities will not meet you anywhere close to halfway. They are incapable of seeing things from your perspective and they don't want to. Though they may profess a willingness to compromise, they won't. It really is not you, and it really has nothing to do with you. While you may be capable of love and forgiveness and kindness, they are not. They are incapable of any meaningful relationships. It really is them.

Showing a predator any emotion is handing them a weapon against you. Indifference from others is their kryptonite. While it may be difficult for you to appear disinterested, it's vital that you seek to achieve that level of control. Also, accepting that the relationship you're in is not really a relationship is pivotal. It's a one-sided pseudo-relationship. Therefore, limiting your expectations and getting out of their sphere of influence as soon as possible is truly in your best interest.

If You Do Choose to Leave

Being in a relationship with a pathological personality will be a roller coaster of ups and downs. You will be blamed for things that aren't your fault. You will find yourself tolerating all kinds of abuse and betrayal. You will be unable to hold onto your good feelings and you will have the energy drained out of you. There are times you will question your own sanity. You only have power over what you decide to do, and over what you say. You do not have power over what a pathological personality decides to do or say.

Many individuals choose to cut ties and leave pathological relationships once they realize that the pathological personality is not going to change in the future.[18] If that's what you decide to do—to leave the relationship—you will need to look out for certain things if you set boundaries, reduce or end contact, or file for divorce.

Keep this in mind: if there was no alliance in the relationship to begin with, you cannot expect there to be one if you are changing the relationship status in any way. When you are dealing with a pathological personality, you have to remind yourself constantly that your thoughts and feelings and concerns fall upon deaf ears and blind eyes.

Any time you choose to alter the relational dynamic with a pathological personality the power differential in the relationship is disrupted and this is something pathological

---

18 Margalis Fjelstad. Stop Caretaking the Borderline or Narcissist: How to End the Drama and Get on with Your Life (Rowman & Littlefield Publishers, Inc., 2014).

personalities can't stand. Be forewarned, if you challenge your pathological partner's perceived authority or sense of entitlement within the relationship, you can expect that emotional abuse and manipulation will increase as your partner seeks to regain control by any means necessary. Pathological partners often resort to threatening to harm themselves or others as a form of coercion and to produce compliance.

If you have minor children with a pathological personality, expect long, drawn-out court involvement, including custody disputes, legal threats, and noncompliance that results in prolonged divorce proceedings with little regard for the wellbeing of the children. You will have to work hard to maintain your own composure in the face of a multitude of predictable legal and interpersonal injustices.

You may also experience hostility from friends and family members related to the pathological partner, or opposition even from your own family. Some pathological personalities will interfere with your relationships with loved ones, friends, and your children, attempting to manipulate them and vilify you while victimizing themselves.

Hope for the best but prepare for the worst. When thwarted, pathological personalities are wired to throw tantrums and escalate drama when they aren't ruling the roost. Throughout the dissolution or separation process, don't focus on the negative things they're saying—they will say whatever they think will work best in the moment to get their way. They often don't remember all of their threats, so don't remind them. Hold on tightly to yourself and your truth even when being provoked. Disentangling yourself from a disordered personality is a lot like waiting for a storm to pass. It may be prolonged, but it *will* eventually pass.

Chapter Seven

Healing and Recovering from TCD

Start with Core Beliefs

Many self-help books actually complicate things for victims of pathological relationship abuse rather than simplify things. Simple is not just better, it's more effective. Simplification begins with beliefs.

The core belief system refers to a set of deeply held assumptions and beliefs that individuals hold about themselves, about others, and about the world, which act as a foundational lens through which they perceive and interact with their environment. Essentially, a core belief system is the underlying framework that shapes a person's self-image and worldview. Often formed early in life, the core belief system can be hijacked and manipulated through pathological relationship abuse, which alters and influences behavior and emotions significantly.

While the rhythm of the disordered dance might be familiar to you as a result of your upbringing or due to previous relationship experiences, processing your past trauma or reviewing your attachment style or examining your adverse childhood experiences will not help you dismantle the trauma bond or alleviate the symptoms of traumatic cognitive dissonance. No matter how many therapists want to lead you down the distant-past path, that's not the best way to get to where you need to go *right now*. In fact, it's a waste of time.

You can revisit those past wounds once you're no longer trauma bonded. Once your nervous system is stabilized and you are back at the controls of your core belief system, you can pursue all the big picture help you want. But to free yourself from a disordered personality, you'll need to focus first on readjusting your core beliefs.

What You *Must* Do First

All journeys, including the journey of recovery, begin with a few first steps, no matter how faltering they might be. Your first step is to identify the beliefs about yourself that developed through the coercion and covert manipulation process. These are the things that your pathological partner convinced you of during the course of your relationship which are <u>not</u> true. False beliefs are a bit like false memories: they're implanted but they bear no resemblance to the truth.

Ask yourself what false beliefs you might be harboring. Those beliefs concerning your relational dynamic and your contributions to it are misbelief hotspots that you will need to examine closely and reconstruct as necessary. In fact, these toxic misbeliefs need to be uprooted and plucked out of your core belief system as well as your autonomic nervous system immediately.

New beliefs that are accurate about yourself, about the pathological person that you were involved with, and about your relational dynamics with them, need to be emotionally and cognitively installed into two distinct places—into your autonomic nervous system and into your core belief system. Ironically, what you must do to achieve this is to first accept the things you do <u>not</u> have to work on.

Traits That Break the Trauma Bond

The following are the traits you'll want to foster within yourself in order to recover from traumatic cognitive dissonance and to dismantle a trauma bond. A major step in breaking free from someone with a trait deficiency disorder, which is essentially what a personality disorder is, is to combat *their* deficiencies with adaptive qualities and characteristics *you* have that they don't. Though you may not know it, you already have these within you.

The disordered personality wants you to engage in their drama, but you can use your adaptive personality characteristics to become indifferent to their attempts to hook you into future drama. You can become immune *enough* to their pathology by rediscovering your own abilities and remembering you have characteristics that they don't have. Your mental and emotional toolkit is much more sophisticated and versatile than theirs. You just have to work on enhancing it.

Here's a list of the contents of your trauma-bond-busting toolkit that you will want to take full advantage of:

Bravery. Within you is the mental and moral strength to face your fears and challenges.

Courage. Within you is the ability to do something that terrifies you; to show strength in the face of pain or grief.

Confidence. Within you is the awareness and certainty of your power and effectiveness.

Goal-Directedness. Within in you is the capacity to maintain a coherent and meaningful forward motion for both short-term and lifelong goals. This requires productive self-reflection and constructive standards to maintain the course.

Humor. Within you is a state of mind or way of being that incorporates a sense of amusement and lightheartedness.

Identity. Within you is stability of self-esteem, accuracy of self-appraisal, regulation of emotional experiences, a positive self-image, and a lifestyle and life course that has purpose and is consistent with one's values, beliefs, wants, and needs.

Intentionality. Within you is the ability to be deliberative and purposeful rather than passive and inconsistent. Within you is a state of being that is directed toward something rather than being a passive receiver of something.

Intuition. Within in you is the superpower of listening to your instincts and responding with your own wealth-pool of natural knowledge and insight rather than reacting to something outside of yourself.

Inventiveness. Within you is the gift of being creative, open to inspiration, innovative, and imaginative.

Optimism. Within you is the will to embrace a sense of hopefulness and confidence about the future and the successful outcome of things.

Persistence. Within you is the strength to press forward in a course of action despite difficulty or opposition.

Resilience. Within you is the power to recover from difficulties regardless of the circumstances.

Five Things *Not* to Focus on

The key five things that you don't have to focus on when you are seeking to unchain yourself from your abuser may surprise you because they are favored topics of many self-help books, which is why they may sound very familiar.

1. **Codependency.** Codependency is a term that has become muddled in misinformation in popular media. The term codependency was originally intended to describe

> how the life of someone closely connected to an addict is also severely affected by the addiction even though that person is not afflicted with an addiction themselves. While the addict is dependent on drugs or alcohol, their significant other becomes "co-dependent" because their life is essentially controlled and ruled by the addiction of their partner. Essentially, they stop living their own life and begin existing simply to accommodate the addict. This further enables the addictive behavior.[19]

Codependency is now being mis-applied to refer to a person with low self-esteem, weak boundaries, lack of trust, and control issues, etc. None of this is accurate. A lot of people have these issues, but codependent is not what they are, unless they are also in a relationship with an addict. It is likewise not true that you are codependent if you ended up with a disordered personality. In fact, the majority of people who are abused by disordered personalities do not identify as codependent.

---

[19] George K. Simon Jr., Character Disturbance: The Phenomenon of Our Age (Parkhurst Brothers Publishers, 2011).

2. **Attachment Style.** Regardless of your attachment style or attachment pattern, a disordered personality will not be stopped from violating your boundaries, your rights, and the standards of prosocial behavior. Your attachment style has no bearing on your susceptibility to predation from manipulative disordered personalities.

3. **Empathy.** This term comes from the translation of a German psychological term, "Einfűhlung," coined in the early nineteenth century, translated as "feeling in." In recent years, the term "empath" has become popular in science fiction to describe a person or being with the paranormal ability to apprehend the mental or emotional state of another individual.

Empathy is a complex capability that enables us to identify and understand the emotional states of others, resulting in compassionate behavior from us to others. Empathy is also the experience of emotional and even physical pain and stress when we witness suffering in others. Empirical studies that assess empathic traits have concluded that, for the most part, people tend to have the most empathy for others who have suffered in a similar way and for those with whom they share a common goal.

There are those who believe that reducing your capacity for empathy will fortify you against an emotional assault from a disordered personality. This is simply not true. First off, empathy is a not a superpower that some people are in touch with constantly. You have sufficient empathy if you have the ability to identify with the feelings and needs of others. You don't need less of this. If you truly believe that you have too much empathy, it's likely that it's not empathy that is the underlying mechanism at work. It could be high levels of anxiety, hypervigilance or hyperawareness due to unresolved trauma or stress, or high neuroticism. True empathy is not something you ever want to reduce.

4. **Boundaries.** Boundaries in relationships are invisible lines that mark limits. These are not concrete blockades; they are merely theoretical "wish lines" you've drawn in the sand. If you are dealing with a disordered personality, boundaries will be violated. They are not enforceable on your end. Strengthening them by being

adamant about their existence won't prevent the disordered personality from walking right through them at will.

5. **Communication.** Even if you are a superb communicator, communicating with a pathological person will go nowhere. Contrary to popular belief, communication is rarely the cause of conflict in healthy relationships. The main problem in relationships actually comes down to perception—one's perception of another's intentions. With a pathological partner, no matter how well you communicate, nothing will be resolved or will change because their perception is skewed by their own excessive self-interest with no regard for the feelings and needs of others.

Five Things You Do Need to Focus on

The key five things that you do have to focus on when you are seeking to unchain yourself from your abuser may also surprise you because they may seem a bit counterintuitive when compared to favored topics of many self-help books.

1. **Unforgiveness.** Give yourself permission to be *unwilling* to forgive your partner if they have not changed or if they have not accepted responsibility for what they've done to you. It's okay not to forgive.

2. **Righteous Anger.** Anger that is properly controlled is righteous anger. This kind of anger is essential for healing because it's likely been suppressed or ignored for far too long. Your anger has most likely been tamped down by fear and sadness so now is the time to be righteously pissed off (in an appropriate manner) about what you've been through.

3. **False Assumptions.** You need to stop assuming that the disordered person in your life knows what you mean when you speak. No matter how articulately you express yourself, they won't have any interest in processing what you have to say, especially about how you feel or what you believe to be true.

4. **Lose Your Expectations.** In terms of the disordered person in your life, have no expectations whatsoever. Don't expect what you can't expect.

5. **Accept That It Won't Change.** It's important to accept that your partner won't change. If they were going to change, they would have already changed.

Chapter Eight

Let's Get To Work

Using Your Imagination

The imagination is often utilized as a treatment tool in psychotherapy and a technique for personal development and self-improvement. Some forms of exposure therapy, for example, involve directing an individual to use their imagination to recall and confront their fears. Specifically, they are instructed to vividly imagine the object of their fear, whether it be a person, place, thing, situation, or activity. This is called *imaginal exposure.*

Neuroscience has revolutionized our understanding of how we can use imaginal exposure. It comes down to this: Because we can use our imagination to recreate something that feels bad, we can just as easily use our imagination to create something new that feels good. Neuroscience has proven that this is possible. By using our imagination to intentionally get in touch with feeling good instead of using it to intentionally feel bad, we can feel better. We can even learn to feel neutral or indifferent about things we've been conditioned to feel bad about. This won't happen overnight, but it will happen with enough effort and practice. Imaginal exposure is an extraordinary technique we can use to get in touch with the balance and neutrality that we want and deserve.

You Must Imagine with Good Intentions

Creating thoughts that are in perfect alignment with positive emotion can be achieved simply by working with your imagination. Your goal is simple: to intentionally feel good right now. Ironically, feeling good doesn't come after you get what you want, although that is what most people think. Yes, you may feel good for a short period of time, but that kind euphoria is nothing more than a sort of "sugar high" that will vanish quickly. Nothing desirable that you achieve or obtain is going to make you feel good permanently.

For example, let's say there is a goal you have your heart set on achieving. If you can't feel good *right now* about that future goal, you won't be able to feel good for very long after you reach it. In fact, any joy you'd hope to feel by achieving that goal may fall well short of your expectations. This is because you are better at feeling bad than you are at feeling good. At least for now. This is where your imagination can help you.

Using your imagination intentionally is the surest way to experience *right now* what you think you want to experience in the future. This is because we truly *feel* whatever we truly *believe*, and the difference-maker when it comes to our beliefs actually lies within the power of our imagination.

When I use the word "imagination," I'm not referring to fantasy, daydreaming or wishful thinking. I'm referring to the literal definition of what it means to imagine. I'm referring to the action of forming new ideas, beliefs, and concepts that are currently not present to the senses. In terms of feeling good, the future is now. You can create a completely positive experience with your imagination right at this moment. And I am going to show you how.

Finding Your *Now*

Try this: imagine a scenario that you truly want to happen—one that is completely void of any negativity. It is important that what you imagine has absolutely no negative associations whatsoever. Other than that, the sky is the limit. Have fun with it.

Take your time. Imagine being filled with positive feelings, as if you have *already* received whatever it is that you want in the scenario you have imagined. Involve as many of your senses as you can. Make sure to relax your body during this exercise by releasing any muscle tension. Breathe deeply. Relax your eyes. Savor the moment. Feel good.

Whenever you imagine something happening, it's happening now. Imagination operates in the present tense, not the future tense. You may imagine your favored scenario is taking place in the future, but your body feels the positive effects in the now. Even if you were to pull up an old memory, your experience of that past event is happening now, not back when it actually occurred. We can go to extraordinary places in our imagination, but no matter where we go, if our imagination is the vehicle we take to get there, we are there *now*.

Now let yourself drift back into the scene you just imagined as if you are there all over again, reliving every aspect of it: the sights, the sounds, the smells, all the physical sensations. Let yourself sink into the rich sensory experience of the scene one more time as if nothing else matters except being there.

Using the power of your imagination on command will help you to get in touch with what it actually feels like to create beliefs that work for you rather than against you. Mastering the practice of imaginal exposure through mental rehearsal will allow you to create new beliefs that can and will assist you in dissolving any trauma bond. In fact, later on, when I review the most evidence-based interventions for recovering from traumatic cognitive dissonance, you will see that they are all rooted in creating new core beliefs that work for you and that overpower the core beliefs that are working against you.

Core Beliefs and the Power of Permission

Recovery, to a large degree, depends on your expectations. Even when it comes to healing from trauma, in order for you to achieve the results you want it's important for you to be aware of your expectations. If you have doubts about being able to recover or heal, those self-doubts or *blocking beliefs* may very well result in you coming to a standstill. It's like swimming against the current. If you resist what you want even the slightest bit you will only get more of what you don't want.

Giving yourself permission to heal is how you swim *with* the current. So get out of your own way by creating new beliefs and new concepts and new meanings that will work for you rather than against you.

The Fallacy of Forgiveness

Forgiveness is complicated and, accordingly, the definition and process of forgiveness varies. How we define it today is different from how it has been used historically. Originally, forgiveness was only granted to someone who has wronged someone and who is aware that their wrongdoing caused harm. Furthermore, to ask for forgiveness, the wrongdoer must accept responsibility for the harm they have done. We are not supposed to grant forgiveness to an offender who fails to acknowledge their wrongdoing. By this definition, therefore, forgiveness cannot be granted to a disordered personality because they don't accept responsibility for their wrongdoing and they don't acknowledge or even care about the harm they've caused others.

While our modern understanding of forgiveness doesn't place so much emphasis on the attitude of the offender, by not requiring an offender to be contrite and show genuine remorse, the healing process of the person who has suffered may be stunted or curtailed. Trying to cast a social predator in a positive light in order to try to forgive them can actually re-traumatize you.

What victims of abuse need to do is become indifferent to the person who caused them harm. They need to become desensitized to the impact of the trauma by participating in healing and recovery practices that actually work. This is much more productive and healing than trying to forgive someone who hasn't earned forgiveness.

Frankly, the concept of forgiveness in our modern age is complicated. Forgiving somebody doesn't mean that you have accepted what they've done and don't have any negative feelings for them anymore. Forgiveness should not be some sort of Get Out Of Jail Free card that we hand out to our transgressors.

Psychological studies and research will tell you that the act of forgiveness is good for your health. But not always. You don't have to forgive your abuser, whether it's a parent or a partner or even your own child. If you don't want to forgive them, don't. Forgiveness is not necessary for healing.

Forgiveness is a transcendent experience that can be reexamined after the trauma has been successfully removed from your nervous system. But we are talking about getting your brain and nervous system back on your side. To do this, you can't be confused or feel guilty about the legitimate anger you feel toward your abuser. Even the revenge fantasies you may have are perfectly normal. To sum it up, if you want to forgive, that's okay. If you don't want to forgive, that is also totally okay.

Meditation Isn't for Every Situation

Not all nervous systems desire or require meditation. When dealing with traumatic cognitive dissonance, some bodies need an energy boost rather than more relaxation. A chronic freeze response often can feel like you are on the verge of fainting. And what do you do when someone faints? You slap their cheeks. You shake them. Sometimes you put ammonia under their nose. What you don't do to someone who has almost fainted is try to get them to meditate.

Sometimes relaxation is just not appropriate and it would be better to sidetrack yourself with exercise or something that requires physical or mental effort of a distracting nature rather than something that requires direct concentration and reflection. The idea that distracting oneself is a copout or is an unhealthy or immature defense mechanism is a myth based on pseudo-psychology theories. If anyone has convinced themselves that they don't need distractions from time to time, they are in denial. Try exercising, cooking, kickboxing, crocheting, singing, dancing—anything that requires movement and energy. If you feel uneasy in the silence or uncomfortable when sitting or lying down, get yourself moving in some way. And add a soundtrack to it. Your brain responds to music in much the same way that it responds to the thought of your favorite dessert or some other guilty sensory pleasure (songs with revenge lyrics, by the way, are fun to listen to and totally appropriate and harmless).

Chapter Nine

The Next Step

"No Contact" Does Not Break a Trauma Bond

We have touched on this briefly already but it's important to reiterate that "No Contact" is not a cure-all. There is a prevailing myth that once a victim of pathological relationship abuse has initiated "no contact" with their ex or former abusive partner, then the trauma bond is broken, or will break eventually. The sad reality is that many survivors who have had no contact with their former pathological partners are still trauma-bonded to their former abuser, even years or decades later.

As a result of the chronic manipulation and denial of responsibility on the part of a pathological partner, victims of pathological relationship abuse can be stuck in a "non-recovery" mode regardless of how long they have gone no contact. This is because the unique trauma that results from pathological abuse will not heal on its own. This trauma will remain present and unresolved until certain trauma processing interventions are put in motion.

No Need for Rationality

Neuroscience has taught us that it is impossible to overcome emotion through rational thinking because human beings are not designed to be rational thinkers while enduring abuse or trauma of any kind. Physical and emotional *feeling* run the show when threat is taking place, not rationality. No decision you make is free from the way you feel, and what you feel does not always have to seem rational to you and certainly not to others. You can try your best to be a so-called "rational" human being when you are suffering from abuse, but it won't happen. Not in this lifetime. The very cells in your body are still sad, hurt, pissed off, terrified, and tormented. The key is to take care of your cells and to not focus on other people's judgments about your suffering. You need to *feel your way* into becoming regulated rather than trying to *think your way* to regulating your so-called "irrational"—but very real and very prevalent—feelings.

"Rationality" is the sense of being in control and, especially, of matching our sensory input with our internal feelings. Accurate predictions about our environment and our experiences with minimal ambiguity are what feel rational. We seek the ability to control our world and create our own sense of safety whenever we please, and we prefer feeling pleasant to feeling unpleasant and feeling calm as opposed to feeling agitated, regardless of the circumstances. This may be ideal but it isn't always possible, and resisting what *is* in favor of what we *want* can create unnecessary suffering. But there is something to do in the moment: construct an alternative meaning about our bodily sensations. Simply redefine what we are experiencing as something more pleasant than unpleasant. Sounds *too* easy, doesn't it?

When they hear this, my therapy patients and my consulting clients often relate to me that they are discouraged, frustrated and disappointed, especially those who believe their situation is hopeless. I am often met with responses like:

"I have already tried that, and it didn't work."

"If it were that easy, I could do it on my own."

"I know that's what I need to do, but I personally cannot do it. I know other people can, and that's what needs to happen, but *I* simply can't."

After their limiting beliefs are challenged, these individuals further explain themselves.

"I've never really found a way to *immediately* experience relief after I try these self-help techniques or exercises."

"Even when I think of a wonderful thought, I can't just fly away to Neverland and feel better, so these techniques must not work for someone like me."

When someone is convinced they will never get over the pain and fear of abuse, when they have truly convinced themselves that they will be stuck forever, when they believe their situation is a lost cause and that they will have to stay in a relationship that is slowly killing them because they can't leave, or when they insist they will forever pine over the fact that it's over, or when they are convinced they will never love again or feel safe again, solutions always seem untenable.

I have found that using gentle and benign provocation while challenging these limiting beliefs goes a long way. I might say something like, "You make a very good point. Whether you believe you can or you can't feel better about this, you are absolutely right. So what do you prefer to believe?"

So ask yourself that very same question: what do you *prefer* to believe? What you answer may just help you get unstuck.

Grief Can Be Good

Grieving the loss of anything when a threat is still ongoing makes grieving complex and increases suffering unnecessarily. Grief is most productive when the threat is gone. When you grieve, it is important to remind your body and your mind that you are safe to do so. Grieving in a regulated state rather than a threat state may feel like profound sadness but it won't feel like anguish. There is a major difference between the two. Where sadness is a general feeling of unhappiness or sorrow, anguish is characterized by deep suffering and inconsolability.

Yes, you will have to grieve what has been lost. There are no shortcuts around this. But any fear or dread that leads you to avoid grief will only prolong the process and may even get you more stuck in negative affect, in particular, in a state of unpleasantness and agitation.

First make sure your body is relaxed, there is no tension, and then let whatever emotions or feelings you are experiencing rise and fall and pass through you without clinging to any of them. Don't resist the grief. Accept the loss. Feel the pain of the loss.

The Pain Will Subside

Nothing lasts forever, including emotional pain. Many survivors of pathological relationship abuse believe that if they let themselves truly feel their emotions—their pain, their grief—that it is going to last forever. Like their tears are going to start flowing and never stop. This belief is very common; thankfully, it is not true at all.

Marathon runners accept from the outset that their brain has to catch up to their bodily sensations for them to finish the race. They need to practice patience, even when it's physically trying to do so. They feel pain and fatigue early in the race when their body is starting to tire, but if they keep running until the unpleasant feeling goes away, they can keep going. Marathoners ignore what I refer to as their own *argument from affect*—which is their body signaling that they are out of energy and are really too tired to move.

Through experience, runners know that all they have to do is keep going until their brain takes charge.

You can use the same principle when you brain is simulating danger via bodily changes and bodily sensations. When the sensory input does not match the predictions your brain made, when your doubts have you feeling you're in danger when you're not, this is also *argument from affect*. You are basing your interpretation of your situation on how pleasant or unpleasant you feel or how calm or agitated you feel rather than basing it on how pleasant or unpleasant you can *make* yourself feel or how calm or agitated you can *make* yourself feel.

Once you *know* that you are safe but you still *feel* unsafe, simply accept that this is because it takes your brain longer to catch up. So, like the marathon runner, keep going despite the unpleasant perception or feeling until it goes away. And ignore your brain's argument from affect that insists you should avoid feeling the unpleasantness. Go ahead and feel the unpleasantness—just keep going until it dissipates. Your feelings about anything are solely based upon whatever your brain believes, so once your brain "catches up," your feelings will too.

What You Can Do for Yourself Right Now

One thing that is very helpful is creating mental and emotional concepts that sustain adaptive and helpful beliefs. Though this might sound more theoretical than practical, you will be able to concretize your beliefs to match your needs. The process, whether contemplative or pragmatic, can even be enjoyable. For example:

- Embark on a mental journey or quest for the "internal" justice that will regulate your life after the abuse regardless of the abuser's lack of accountability and denial of responsibility.
- Adapt your habits of mind to that regulating factor of internal justice.
- Build yourself up with empowering mental concepts from your personal code of integrity.
- Refrain from avoiding the reality of the circumstances. We either adapt or we die.
- Use your circumstances as opportunities or aids in your progress.

- Use your circumstances to discover the possibilities within yourself.

Don't Seek to Become a Human Lie Detector

I often get asked by survivors, "how can I be sure the next person I get involved with is not just like the person I was deceived by?" What they are looking for is a way to get better at detecting narcissists and psychopaths and borderlines in the world. They hope to be able to identify specific *tells* so that, forearmed with knowledge and with practice, they can become skilled at identifying manipulative people.

The truth is you can't *always* rely on your gut instincts or your intuition alone to reveal the truth about someone. What you need to do is learn to *listen for disorder* when you are getting to know someone; that is, you must pay attention to what's *not* there, what's missing. Deception is about absence, not presence. In the early stages of dating or in collaborating with someone, ask yourself whether the interaction lines up with your expectations rather than try to detect lies. Seeking to identify inconsistencies is actually a better strategy than trying to become a mind reader.

The truth is there will never be a shortcut to absolutely determine if you are being duped or deceived by another individual. Experts are not immune to being fooled, and there is no such thing as a foolproof lie detector that you can install in your brain or nervous system to be completely immune to deception.

The good news is you don't have to become a human lie detector to keep yourself safe and prevent future abuse. You only need to become skilled at recognizing inconsistencies. Your earned knowledge that disordered people exist gives you a distinct advantage.

Chapter Ten

Seeking Help

Keep this in mind: it is completely normal to struggle with feelings of guilt, anxiety, fear, confusion, uncertainty, exhaustion, and internal conflict when seeking help and understanding about a relationship that involves pathological abuse.

One Size Doesn't Fit All

The truth is there isn't one perfectly right way to recover from pathological relationship abuse. There are, however, enough ways to systematically approach the symptoms of traumatic cognitive dissonance to challenge and change core beliefs. Pathological relationship trauma symptoms, including unresolved traumatic cognitive dissonance, can be resolved with treatment. But not just any treatment:

trauma-informed treatment that specifically targets the pathological relationship abuse rather than the victim's childhood experiences or their attachment style is what is required. Treatment should include education—based on science, not pop-psychology or outdated theories—on personality disorders and pathological partners, and a corrective emotional experience under the guidance of a professional that a victim/survivor can really trust. Rigid, general interventions and therapeutic protocols that focus on in-depth explorations of your childhood experiences, however, tend to be unhelpful.

There is no one-size fits all intervention that results in an ideal outcome for everyone. The way your brain and body respond to an intervention will not be identical to the way someone else's brain and body responds. You might need to learn how to read your body and your mind more accurately during the process of healing and recovery for optimal results.

The Difficulty in Finding Effective Professional Support

If you've sought help in the past and it was ineffective it is likely this was because the professional was not aware of the distinct trauma symptoms that result from TCD and attempted to treat pathological relationship abuse using traditional methods based on classical theory, cognitive theory, insight-oriented theory, or tried to treat you based on your childhood experiences, attachment style, etc., none of which address pathological relationship abuse. Traditional interventions often make assumptions about brain and nervous system functioning that have been discredited by more recent scientific research. Many classical views of psychology presume the nervous system is not hijacked and that adaptive, flexible sensory information processing is still "online" and is not compromised. The truth of the matter is if you are in a chronic stress state, it may not always be possible to consciously think and reason your way out of perceiving threat. You need to experience systemic regulation and relaxation <u>before</u> you can restore your flexibility of belief.

While childhood trauma, domestic violence, and abuse within the context of previous relationships are relevant to core beliefs and do require attention, these aspects of your experience should <u>not</u> be the focus when it comes to recovering from trauma bonds and traumatic cognitive dissonance resulting from pathological relationship abuse. Your beliefs within the context of the relationship need to be your priority. Reprocessing and working through your childhood will not free you from the clutches of manipulation. You don't need to "work through" everything you've ever been through to feel better. This is a myth.

With survivors of cults, for example, the victim is removed from the clutches of the cult first. Once they are back to a reasonable level of regulated functioning then a discussion can ensue concerning any vulnerabilities that may have made them a target of the cult in the first place. The same goes for survivors of disordered personalities.

Why Professional Help Can Fail or Prove Ineffective

Too many mental health professionals don't specialize in personality disorders and so don't fully understand the impact of personality pathology on relationships and other people. Also, many have a resistance to explicitly establishing scientific criteria for treatment efficacy.[20] In addition, many assume all forms of abuse and relationship dysfunction are created equal and are mutually created, believing falsely that it takes two to tango.

Many mental health professionals view personality pathology—if they recognize it—as "neurodivergence," which can simply be a softened way of saying that disordered personalities are simply diverse in a benign sort of way and that there really is no such thing as "normal." This is almost akin to saying that personality disorders don't exist. They point to environmentally learned behavioral conditions or symptomatic conditions that stem from complex or developmental trauma as explanations for why such personalities behave as they do, though nothing can be further from the truth. Because of this fallacious thinking, many professionals approach treatment of all clients using person-centered/humanistic perspectives or psychodynamic perspectives that completely

---

20 Carol Tavris, "The Scientist-Practitioner Gap: Revisiting 'A View from the Bridge' a Decade Later," in The Science and Pseudoscience of Clinical Psychology, ed. Scott O. Lilienfeld, Steven J. Lynn, and Jeffrey M. Lohr, 2nd ed. (The Guilford Press, 2015), ix-xx.

overlook or dismiss the reality of the biological basis of behavior.

If, on the other hand, a mental health professional does acknowledge that personality disorders exist, a common automatic assumption is that the disordered person is a victim of severe trauma, abuse, or neglect, and their pathology is just a "reenactment" of what happened to them. This is false.

And then there is the pervasive and well-meaning view in the mental health professional community that all human beings are basically the same on the inside. By assuming that even pathological personalities are treatable, can be reasoned with, and are collaborative, this creates a false equivalency between the victim and their abuser. They focus on any attributes of the pathological personality's "sameness," especially on their desire for relationships. But a disordered personality who seeks a relationship is not doing so for bonding purposes. They are doing so to find a victim.

Also, many mental health professionals hold theory biases that cause harm to their clients because these biases may blind them to the reality of personality pathology. While harboring under this misassumption, they can't adequately educate survivors on the kind of relationship they are actually in. In turn, they cannot sufficiently validate survivors and help them recover from the unique form of trauma that results from pathological relationship abuse. In the worst case scenario, the victim is blamed by the person they sought help from for causing the problem in the first place.

EMDR as an Effective Trauma Treatment

Eye Movement Desensitization And Reprocessing Therapy (EMDR) is a type of trauma treatment that targets and reprocesses traumatic memories as well reduces intrusive and negative thoughts, feelings, and beliefs about trauma. The great thing about EMDR is that it tackles past and present trauma triggers but also helps you prepare for future trauma exposure. EMDR has been shown to be extremely effective at treating single incident traumas, developmental trauma, and complex trauma resulting from attachment relationships. This is accomplished because EMDR somehow, someway, seems to unlock and grant access to stuck thoughts, feelings, and beliefs that keep you in non-recovery mode, allowing the brain and nervous system to adaptively process traumatic experiences the way it processes any other experience.

Scientific literature on EMDR has produced a number of conclusions:

- EMDR is an efficacious treatment for trauma
- The efficacy is comparable to that of Prolonged Exposure Therapy
- The efficacy is comparable to that of Anxiety Management Training (Stress Inoculation)
- The efficacy is comparable to that of Cognitive Processing Therapy[21]

Despite its tremendous effectiveness, there are some potential hiccups to the use of EMDR. First, an ideal level of adaptive belief (buy in) in the process seems to be necessary for optimal results. Second, trauma processing can be blocked or inhibited if your fear of facing what needs to be faced is too powerful. Trauma processing can

---

21 Jeffrey M. Lohr et al., "Science- and Non-Science-Based Treatments for Trauma-Related Stress Disorders," in The Science and Pseudoscience in Clinical Psychology, ed. Scott O. Lilienfeld, Steven J. Lynn, and Jeffrey M. Lohr, 2nd ed. (The Guilford Press, 2015), 277-321.

also be blocked by inaccurate beliefs related to responsibility, safety, and choice that have yet to be identified. Lastly, new information and new perspectives might need to come "online" before processing is fully effective.

Bilateral Stimulation

EMDR utilizes a technique known as bilateral stimulation or bilateral activation to unlock traumatic memories that are trapped in the past and intruding upon the present. Bilateral stimulation activates the brain and autonomic nervous system in such a way that allows adaptive information to replace traumatic information. Because certain types of traumas deactivate the brain and the nervous system's natural ability to process information in a positive way, this technique reactivates your natural ability to process information in a way that is helpful to you.

Bilateral stimulation has been shown to be highly effective for dismantling trauma bonds and for alleviating symptoms of traumatic cognitive dissonance when the beliefs about oneself, one's pathological partner and the relationship as a whole are identified, challenged, targeted, and modified to reestablish the perceptual reality that has been distorted by the pathological person who manipulated those beliefs in the first place. This is a completely separate process from addressing any other past trauma or relationship patterns and dynamics and must be targeted first and separately in order for resolution to occur.

Applying bilateral stimulation while focusing on distressing events from the past, present, and future has been shown to:

- Reduce threat responses related to traumatic events or perceived danger.
- Reduce the level of distress when recalling a traumatic memory or when preparing for a future distressing event.
- Reduce the need to avoid thoughts, feelings, situations, and places related to past, present, and future potential distressing events.
- Activate the adaptive mode of the parasympathetic nervous system.
- Desensitize intense images of a traumatic memory.
- Eliminate flashbacks and nightmares.

- Create new neural pathways that work to resolve contradictory core beliefs and dissolve traumatic cognitive dissonance.

Other Evidence-Based Interventions

Evidence-based therapy focuses on helping us lessen our struggle by using strategies and action steps such as *psychological flexibility* and *acceptance*. When we can decrease our need to "get rid" of uncomfortable feelings and thoughts and learn to notice them, experience them, but not always believe what our mind tells us, we can feel better.

Prolonged Exposure (PE). This is a form of treatment that helps individuals confront memories and feelings that are typically avoided. PE helps people learn that memories and reminders of trauma are not dangerous, and that distress does not last forever. During treatment, an individual will learn about Post Traumatic Stress Disorder (PTSD) and participate in "in vivo" and "imaginal" exercises. PE is considered one of the most if not the most effective treatments for PTSD, and most people who complete the treatment show a noticeable improvement in symptoms.

Stress Inoculation. This form of treatment reduces symptoms of anxiety, irritability, and hyperarousal. The techniques employed include: Psychoeducation, which is learning about trauma and the responses to it that occur; Relaxation Training, which is the reduction of muscle tension since stress cannot really exist in a relaxed body; Self-Instruction, which is learning how to how to mentally solve problems while alone, in particular by employing a modification of maladaptive expectations of danger, beliefs about inability to control stressors and other inaccuracies in interpretations regarding the nature and occurrence of stress, past or present.

Cognitive Processing (CPT). CPT is one of the most researched treatments for PTSD and is strongly recommended by clinical practice guidelines. It's been shown to be effective in treating PTSD that develops after a variety of traumatic events, including child abuse, sexual assault, and relationship abuse.

CPT is a 12-session treatment that teaches patients how to identify and change unhelpful thoughts that can contribute to PTSD. The goal is to create a new understanding of the traumatic event or events so that it doesn't have such a negative impact on the patient's current life.

During CPT, patients learn about common changes in beliefs that can occur after trauma, such as changes in how they feel about safety, trust, power, and self-esteem. They also learn to find a balance between their pre- and post-trauma beliefs. Patients may write about their traumatic experiences and complete practice assignments to apply what they're learning.[22]

Accelerated Resolution Therapy (ART)

Accelerated Resolution Therapy (ART) is similar to the EMDR process in that it uses eye movement techniques, but it is a bit more directive in that it guides you to replace the negative images in the mind that cause the symptoms of trauma with positive images of your own choosing. The process is very quick, with clients often finding relief within the very first session. Once the negative images are replaced by positive ones, the trauma triggers and symptoms stop as well.

---

22 Patricia A. Resick, Candice M. Monson, and Kathleen M. Chard, Cognitive Processing Therapy for PTSD: A Comprehensive Manual (The Guilford Press, 2017).

ART is a comfortable choice for clients because it doesn't require talking about any details of the trauma. This makes the therapy much less intimidating for the client.

Chapter Eleven

Exercises

Exercise 1. Those Hurtful Things

As a baseline to refer to, list the things about your partner's behavior that hurt you:

1. ______________________________
2. ______________________________
3. ______________________________
4. ______________________________
5. ______________________________
6. ______________________________
7. ______________________________
8. ______________________________
9. ______________________________
10. ______________________________
11. ______________________________
12. ______________________________
13. ______________________________
14. ______________________________
15. ______________________________
16. ______________________________
17. ______________________________
18. ______________________________
19. ______________________________
20. ______________________________

Exercise 2. Rightful Expectations

Many victims and survivors of pathological relationship abuse who suffer from traumatic cognitive dissonance have difficulty identifying what normal behavior in a relationship looks like. Imagine telling your best friend what twenty qualities and behaviors they have the right to expect from their partner:

1. ________________________________
2. ________________________________
3. ________________________________
4. ________________________________
5. ________________________________
6. ________________________________
7. ________________________________
8. ________________________________
9. ________________________________
10. ________________________________
11. ________________________________
12. ________________________________
13. ________________________________
14. ________________________________
15. ________________________________
16. ________________________________
17. ________________________________
18. ________________________________
19. ________________________________
20. ________________________________

Exercise 3: Rate Yourself

How do you rate your current possession of the following traits (as described in a previous chapter) on a scale of 0-10?

- Bravery 0 1 2 3 4 5 6 7 8 9 10
- Confidence 0 1 2 3 4 5 6 7 8 9 10
- Courage 0 1 2 3 4 5 6 7 8 9 10
- Goal-Directedness 0 1 2 3 4 5 6 7 8 9 10
- Humor 0 1 2 3 4 5 6 7 8 9 10
- Identity 0 1 2 3 4 5 6 7 8 9 10
- Intentionality 0 1 2 3 4 5 6 7 8 9 10
- Intuition 0 1 2 3 4 5 6 7 8 9 10
- Inventiveness 0 1 2 3 4 5 6 7 8 9 10
- Optimism 0 1 2 3 4 5 6 7 8 9 10
- Persistence 0 1 2 3 4 5 6 7 8 9 10
- Resilience 0 1 2 3 4 5 6 7 8 9 10

Exercise 4: Your Code Of Integrity

Your character articulates your integrity and should be made up of qualities that you choose to live by regardless of whether others choose to do so or not. Below is a list of words that can be used to create your own Code of Integrity.

HONEST	CHALLENGING	EFFICIENT	LEADER
FRUGAL	FAITHFUL	HUMOROUS	HOPEFUL
GREEDY	OPTIMISTIC	FEARLESS	CONSERVATIVE
LIBERAL	MODERATE	TOLERANT	ASSERTIVE
OUTSPOKEN	POWERFUL	CONFIDENT	PRODUCTIVE
LOVING	FAIR	STRONG	DETERMINED
EFFECTIVE	CREATIVE	COMPASSIONATE	HONORABLE
RESILIENT	COMMITTED	JOYFUL	PEACEFUL
RESPONSIBLE	COURAGEOUS	RESPECTFUL	UNDERSTANDING
GENEROUS	MOTIVATED	HUMBLE	FOCUSED
COMMITTED	DISCIPLINED	CALM	SECURE

Pick 7 to 10 words from the chart above that resonate the most with you in terms of the qualities and principles you want most to embody. You will use these to build your own Code of Integrity. Make certain that the words you choose are really the right ones for you. Don't make your choices based on the opinions of anyone else or what you think you *should* choose.

SAMPLE CODE OF INTEGRITY

1. I am always **honest** and genuine in my relationships with others
2. I am **committed** to finishing what I start
3. I approach life's challenges, changes, and discomforts with **courage**
4. I am **assertive** in my boundaries with self and others
5. I am **optimistic** about endless possibilities and potentials
6. I am **compassionate** towards myself
7. I am **responsible** for my own thoughts, feelings and actions
8. I am **secure** in my life purpose
9. I am **resilient** in all aspects of life regardless of the circumstances

Now create your own Code of Integrity based on the principles and characteristics you chose above.

1. ______________________________
2. ______________________________
3. ______________________________
4. ______________________________
5. ______________________________
6. ______________________________
7. ______________________________
8. ______________________________
9. ______________________________
10. ______________________________

Exercise 5: Identifying Your Core Beliefs

First, write down the beliefs you held about the kind of person you knew yourself to be before your relationship with a pathological partner. State these beliefs in the form of "I am" statements, like *I am kind. I am capable. I am good enough*, etc. For help with this, see the two lists of common core beliefs about oneself below. You can also reference what the caring and supportive people in your life outside of the pathological relationship have said they believe about you.

Next, write down the beliefs about yourself that have developed during your relationship with a pathological personality. These are beliefs that you did not previously hold about yourself but which began after your exposure to chronic manipulation, conflict, and abuse. Even if you know cognitively that these beliefs are not accurate, they may still *feel* true to you at your core.

Finally, write down any beliefs about yourself that have developed after ties were severed with any pathological personalities in your life even if there is still some necessary contact due to comingled business, finances, community property or shared custody of children, etc.

Common Traumatic Core Beliefs	
I don't deserve to love	I have to be perfect
I don't deserve to be happy	I have to please everyone else
I don't belong	I have to accommodate at my own expense
I don't deserve good things	I have to be strong
I am a bad person	There is no one I can trust
I am worthless	I have no self-control
I am ashamed	I have no way out
I am inadequate	I am trapped
I am broken	I am stuck
I am permanently damaged	I am at fault
I am stupid	I am to blame
I am insignificant	I am not okay
I should have done something different	I am different
I did something wrong	I am flawed
I should have known better	I cannot move forward
I can't trust my judgment	I brought this upon myself
No one believes me	I cannot make mistakes
I cannot protect myself	I cannot control myself
I am not safe	I cannot control my emotions
It's not okay to feel my emotions	I cannot learn from the past
It's not okay to express my emotions	I cannot get over this
I cannot let it out	No one will love me after this
I am not in control	I will always be alone
I am powerless	I will never recover
I am helpless	My pain will last forever
I am weak	I cannot be alone
I cannot get what I want	I am better off dead
I cannot move forward	I am not going to survive

Common Restorative Core Beliefs	
I deserve to love	I can be human
I deserve to be happy	I can put myself first sometimes
I belong	I have can have boundaries
I deserve good things	I can still be vulnerable
I am a good person	There are people I can trust
I am worthy	I have self-control
I am unashamed	I have a way out
I am adequate	I am able to get free
I am whole	I am free
I can heal	I am not at fault
I am smart/competent	I am not to blame for many things
I am significant	I am okay
I did the best I could	I am normal
I did the right thing	I don't need to be perfect
I learned from my experience	I can move forward
I can trust my judgment	I had good intentions
I can trust many people	I can make mistakes
I can protect myself	I can control myself
I am safe/I can create my sense of safety	I can control my emotions
It's okay to feel my emotions	I can learn from the past
It's okay to express my emotions	I can get over this
I can let it out	Someone will love me after this
I am in control	I will find someone to love
I am powerful	I will recover
I can help myself	My pain will subside
I am strong	I can be alone when I need to be
I can get what I want	I have so much to live for
I can move forward	I will survive

Exercise 6: Final Questions to Ask Yourself

At this point in your journey through the pages of this book, you should be able to ask yourself some pertinent self-probing questions that won't be nearly as painful as the self-inquiry would have been in the beginning because by now you will have gained both knowledge and objectivity about the situation you've endured. What's more, by this point you will be able to interpret your answers and glean wisdom from them without any instruction whatsoever and that should feel very good.

- What would you prefer to feel about you if you knew you really can choose how to feel? What would you prefer to feel about you *instead* of what you feel?
- What would you prefer to think about you if you knew you really can choose how to think?
- What would you prefer to believe about you if you knew you really can choose what to believe?
- What do you know is true about the former disordered personality in your life that might not feel true?

- What would you want someone you loved to know about themselves if they were similar to you and went through what you did?
- What would you want someone you loved to know about their partner if their partner was just like yours?
- What would you want someone you love to know about their relationship dynamic if they were in the same relationship you were in and had trouble seeing it clearly for what it is?
- What would you prefer to feel about the relationship if you knew you really can choose how to feel?
- What would you prefer to think about the relationship if you knew you really can choose how to think about it?
- What would you prefer to believe about the relationship if you knew you really can choose what to believe about it?
- Who do you know that deserves what you endured? Anyone? Why?
- Who would you wish what happened to you upon? Why?

Chapter Twelve

Some Final Thoughts

It's Okay to Grieve

You will likely undergo a grieving process related to the abuse you have experienced in the past. You will grieve the loss of the relationship you hoped to have not just in the present but in the future. That's okay. Keep in mind, grieving the loss of anything *while you're perceiving a threat* makes the grieving process complex and increases unnecessary suffering. When you grieve, it is important to remind your body and your brain that you are safe to grieve. Grieving in a relaxed state rather than a threat state will feel like sadness rather than like anguish.

Recovery and Healing

Getting equipped with accurate knowledge and insight regarding pathological relationship abuse is an essential first step in the healing and recovery process. However, it doesn't necessarily mean that you are not going to struggle to make decisions about your relationship.

Recovery and healing require you to get reacquainted with your own values, beliefs, expectations, and assumptions. Oftentimes, we make decisions about relationships, and about life in general, based on beliefs and values we have inherited from others, including our families of origin and the people who mistreat and abuse us. These beliefs and values may have served us well in the past but when it comes to making decisions about pathological relationships, it is vitally important that you allow yourself to be guided by your own beliefs and values, not someone else's.[23]

---

23 Paul T. Mason & Randi Kreger, *Stop Walking on Eggshells: Taking Your Life Back When Someone You Care About Has Borderline Personality Disorder* (New Harbinger Publications, 2020).

Practice Self-Compassion

Many people who have been abused find it extremely difficult to be gentle with themselves and find it quite easy to be hard on themselves. While it's tempting to worry that difficulty with self-compassion is confirmation that there really is something about you that is "unworthy" or "less than" or "not good enough," the truth is that you just haven't sufficiently practiced self-compassion enough for your brain to automatically engage in the process.

Self-compassion doesn't need to involve reciting affirmations or awkwardly hugging oneself or shedding fountains of tears for what you've been through. Self-compassion could just involve recognizing facts about one's qualities and achievements. Think about your good qualities and achievements, take inventory of them, and acknowledge that these qualities and achievements have worth and merit. Celebrate your little victories throughout the day and reward yourself by acknowledging their existence rather than denying their reality. This is a gift you can give yourself, one that you fully deserve.

> You might start with this:
> "Today, I noticed that I (name a small mental, emotional or physical task that you completed or little victory you achieved)__________________, and I can remember the pleasant emotions that I felt at the time, no matter how brief or fleeting." And then "I will remember the wellness feelings that accompanied those moments."

Like life itself, it's the little moments that matter so provide yourself the opportunities for those little moments.

Recovery seldom happens as a big epiphany; healing tends to start slowly, proceed slowly, but ultimately it will last. Traumatic Cognitive Dissonance can be overcome with an understanding of disordered personalities, with self-awareness and self-compassion, and, when needed, with professional help. Traumatic Cognitive Dissonance doesn't have to be a permanent state, unless you let it be. It's your life; you are ultimately in charge of what you believe and how you feel so make it count in your favor.

Journaling

Here are some blank pages for you to jot down your thoughts or notes as needed. Write what you wish—remember, it's whatever makes you happy, however small it might be, that counts as a victory. TCD is fundamentally an unhappy state; ultimately triumphing over it starts with finding sparks of happiness in the moment. This is *your* moment, no one else's.

References

Barrett, L. F. (2018). How emotions are made: The secret life of the brain. Harper.

Brown, S. L., Paradise, C., & Brennan, B. (2021). Intensive training on narcissistic and psychopathic abuse. PESI, Inc. .

Fjelstad, M. (2013). Stop caretaking the borderline or narcissist: How to end the drama and get on with your life. Rowman & Littlefield Publishers, Inc. .

Gentry, J. E. (2021). Forward-facing freedom: Healing the past, transforming the present, a future on purpose. Outskirts Press.

Godwin, A., & Lester, G. W. (2021). Demystifying personality disorders: Clinical skills for working with drama and manipulation. Pesi Publishing.

Herpertz, S. C., & Bertsch, K. (2022). Neuroscience and personality disorders. In S.K. Huprich (Ed.), Personality disorders and pathology:

Integrating clinical assessment and practice in the DSM-5 and ICD-11 era (pp. 323-349). American Psychological Association.

Lohr, J. M., Gist, R., Deacon, B., Devilly, G. J., & Varker, T. (2015). Science-and non-science-based treatments for trauma-related stress disorders. In S.O. Lilienfeld, S. J. Lynn, & J. M. Lohr (Eds.), Science and pseudoscience in clinical psychology (2nd ed., pp. 277-321). The Guilford Press.

Mason, P. T., & Kreger, R. (2020). Stop walking on eggshells: Taking your life back when someone you care about has borderline personality disorder (3rd ed., Rev.). New Harbinger Publications, Inc. .

Mitchell, K. J. (2018). Innate: How the wiring of our brains shapes who we are. Princeton University Press.

Paris, J. (2023). Myths of Trauma: Why adversity does not necessarily make us sick. Oxford University Press.

Plomin, R. (2019). Blueprint: How DNA makes us who we are. The MIT Press.

Ringwald, W. R., Emery, L., Khoo, S., Clark, L. A., Kotelnikova, Y., Scalco, M. D., Watson, D., Wright, A. G., & Simms, L. J. (2023). Structure of pathological personality traits through the lens of the CAT-PD model. Assessment, 30(7), 2276-2295.

Simon, Jr., G. K. (2011). Character disturbance: The phenomenon of our age. Parkhurst Brothers Publishers.

Tavris, C. (2015). The scientist-practitioner gap: Revisiting "a view from the bridge" a decade later. In S.O. Lilienfeld, S.J. Lynn, & J.M. Lohr (Eds.), The science and pseudoscience of clinical psychology (2nd ed., pp. ix-xx). The Guilford Press.

Other Titles by Peter Salerno, PsyD

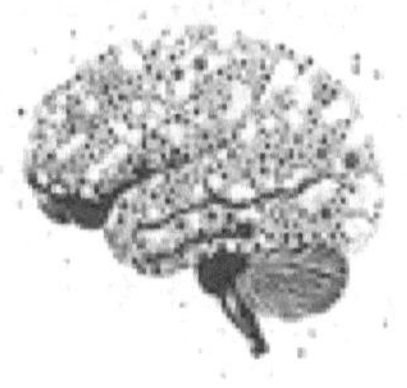

PETER SALERNO, PsyD

What Causes Narcissism?

The world has been indoctrinated with the false notion that narcissism is the result of a bad childhood.

It's as if narcissists have been granted immunity from responsibility. Mental health professionals—and the general public alike—seem more than willing to offer narcissists a perfectly convenient scapegoat: trauma.

The goal of this book, using the most recent empirical evidence on the etiology and treatment of narcissistic personality disorder—is to dispel the widely held and *already* discredited myth that narcissism is the result of childhood trauma. Despite evidence to the contrary, this widely held myth continues to prevail in popular media and culture.

This book aims to correct the mistakes related to the cause of narcissism so that mental health practitioners and the general public will have a scientifically informed understanding of etiology and intervention. Because the reality is that almost everything we have been taught about the cause of narcissism...is *wrong*.

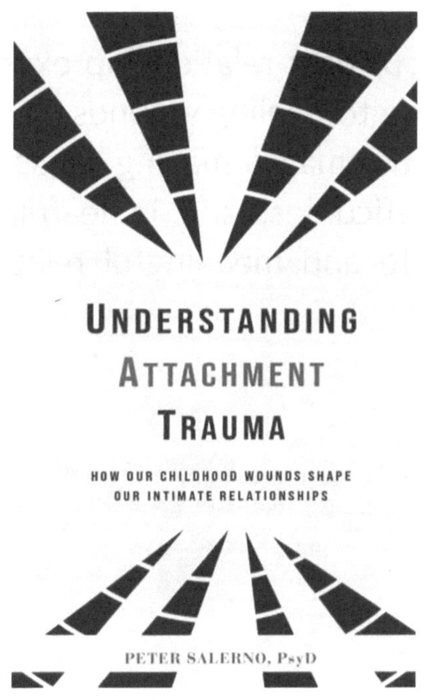

UNDERSTANDING
ATTACHMENT
TRAUMA
HOW OUR CHILDHOOD WOUNDS SHAPE
OUR INTIMATE RELATIONSHIPS
PETER SALERNO, PsyD

Bonding with other people is necessary for survival.

But what happens when attachment fails? Nothing less than trauma. And this is much more common than you might think. Attachment trauma not only affects our daily lives, it also significantly impacts our most intimate relationships in the future.

Because understanding, healing and thriving go hand in hand, this book will not only help you understand how unresolved attachment trauma predicted your past relationship experiences, it is also a guide to healing wounds resulting from attachment trauma, to making sense of present relational difficulties, and in learning how to seek out safe and meaningful relationships in the future.

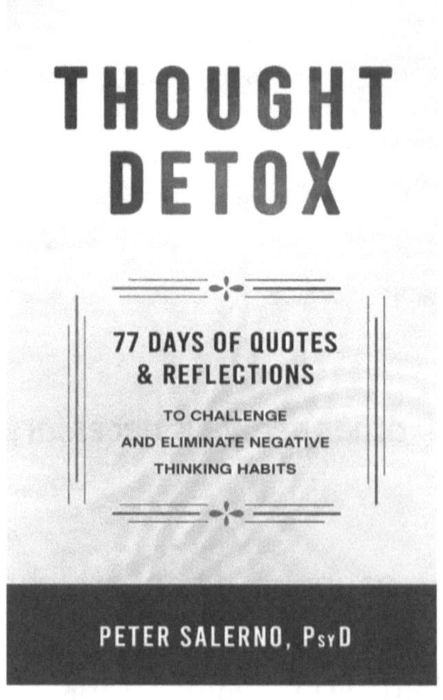

You become what you think about all day long.

-Ralph Waldo Emerson

Thoughts are so much more important than we give them credit for. Thoughts are powerful, and they have a strong influence over our emotions and our actions. Essentially, our thoughts can make us or break us.

Thought Detox condenses a wide range of simple yet brilliant truths and blends them into a concise daily guide accompanied by practical reflections that will help you to challenge thoughts and ideas that are not working for you and that might even be seriously impacting your mental wellbeing and physical health.

With this pocket guide of incredible thoughts and ideas at hand, you are well on your way toward developing better thinking habits that will change your perspective on life for the better while improving your overall health and wellbeing.

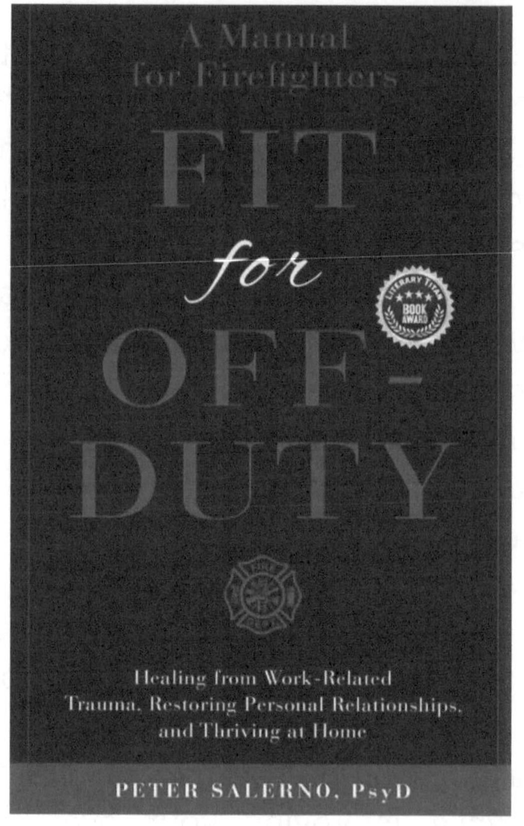

Every firefighter is a trauma survivor. Even veteran firefighters may not realize this. But constant exposure to traumatic events takes a serious toll. The body is affected, so is the nervous system, and so are the firefighter's personal relationships. Off-duty days can become something to dread rather than look forward to. It doesn't need to be this way. This book—written by a trauma therapist from a firefighter family—is a definitive manual for healing from trauma exposure for those who serve in the fire service and for those who love them. Feeling fit, healthy and unburdened by the effects of trauma can be a short-term therapeutic process. And there are steps firefighters can take on their own, immediately. **This book is a good place to start.**

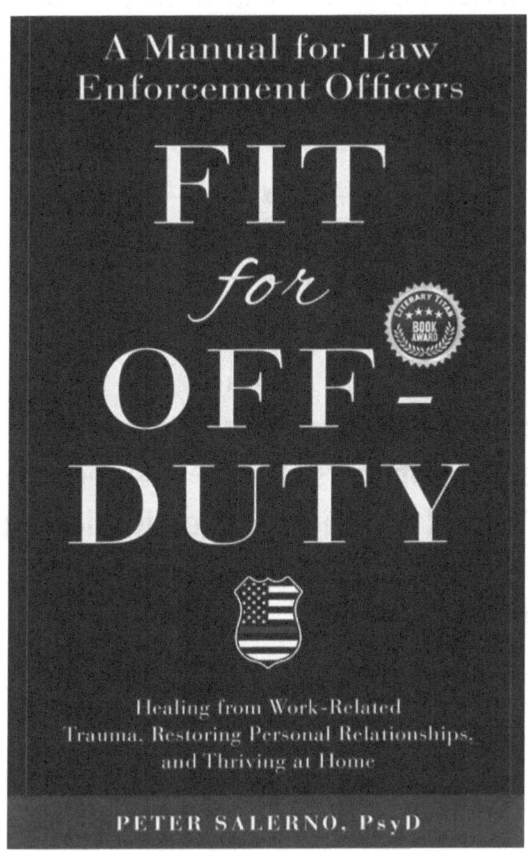

Every Law Enforcement Officer is a Trauma Survivor. Even veteran officers may not realize this. But constant exposure to traumatic events takes a serious toll. The body is affected, so is the nervous system, and so are the officer's personal relationships. Off-duty days can become something to dread rather than look forward to. It doesn't need to be this way. This book—written by a trauma therapist from a first responder family—is a definitive manual for healing from trauma exposure for those who serve in law enforcement and for those who love them. Feeling fit, healthy and unburdened by the effects of trauma can be a short-term therapeutic process. And there are steps law enforcement officers can take on their own, immediately. This book is a good place to start.

***This book is now required reading for law enforcement officers at the FBI Academy, which is the Federal Bureau of Investigation's training and research center for FBI agents in Quantico, Virginia.**

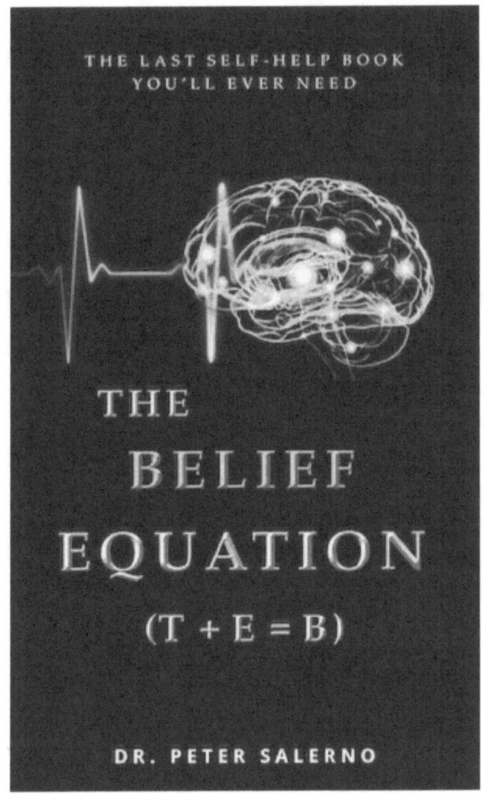

If you want to rid yourself of a negative mindset that keeps you from getting what you want in life, THE BELIEF EQUATION will help you do just that.

Once we consciously program our mind and body to work in our favor rather than against our best interests, we no longer have to accept that we are somehow destined to be someone we don't want to be.

By learning to program yourself to influence your waking consciousness, as well as how you act and behave, you will be able to automatically live life on your terms without even having to think!

If there is any aspect of your life that you are currently not satisfied with, this book will show you how to get everything you want. All you have to do is solve The Belief Equation.

Made in United States
Troutdale, OR
03/24/2025

29992544R00121